Achieving Results

Achieving Results

Maximizing Student Success in the Schoolhouse

Nicholas D. Young,
Kristen Bonanno-Sotiropoulos,
and Jennifer A. Smolinski

ROWMAN & LITTLEFIELD
Lanham • Boulder • New York • London

Published by Rowman & Littlefield
A wholly owned subsidiary of The Rowman & Littlefield Publishing Group, Inc.
4501 Forbes Boulevard, Suite 200, Lanham, Maryland 20706
www.rowman.com

Unit A, Whitacre Mews, 26-34 Stannary Street, London SE11 4AB

Copyright © 2018 by Nicholas D. Young, Kristen Bonanno-Sotiropoulos, and Jennifer A. Smolinksi

All rights reserved. No part of this book may be reproduced in any form or by any electronic or mechanical means, including information storage and retrieval systems, without written permission from the publisher, except by a reviewer who may quote passages in a review.

British Library Cataloguing in Publication Information Available

Library of Congress Cataloging-in-Publication Data

Names: Young, Nicholas D., 1967- author. | Bonanno-Sotiropoulos, Kristen, author. | Smolinksi, Jennifer A., author.
Title: Achieving results : maximizing student success in the schoolhouse / Nicholas D. Young, Kristen Bonanno-Sotiropoulos, and Jennifer A. Smolinksi.
Description: Lanham, Maryland : Rowman & Littlefield, [2018] | Includes bibliographical references.
Identifiers: LCCN 2018002233 (print) | LCCN 2018016075 (ebook) | ISBN 9781475842289 (electronic) | ISBN 9781475842265 (cloth : alk. paper) | ISBN 9781475842272 (pbk. : alk. paper)
Subjects: LCSH: Academic achievement—United States. | Effective teaching—United States. | Teachers—In-service training—United States. | Education—Parent participation—United States. | Community and school—United States.
Classification: LCC LB1062.6 (ebook) | LCC LB1062.6 .Y68 2018 (print) | DDC 371.26/4—dc23
LC record available at https://lccn.loc.gov/2018002233

♾™ The paper used in this publication meets the minimum requirements of American National Standard for Information Sciences—Permanence of Paper for Printed Library Materials, ANSI/NISO Z39.48-1992.

Printed in the United States of America

Nicholas D. Young

I wish to dedicate this tome to my daughter, Melanie. She graduated from American International College this past spring, earning a bachelor of arts with the highly coveted summa cum laude designation, and I could not be more proud of what she has accomplished. This book is focused on achieving educational results. Melanie has demonstrated the role the individual student can play in making that happen. She earned high marks from kindergarten through college by devoting the time and effort needed to be successful every day, month, and year of her illustrious academic career. It is not surprising that Melanie is now working long hours at a local hospital to gain the practical experience she needs to continue on to graduate school. I have no doubt that she will earn whatever graduate degrees she so desires in the coming years. At the tender age of twenty-one, she is modeling the common phrase frequently quoted by her grandfather: "The harder you work, the luckier you become." May Melanie know that her dad loves her and that our whole family wishes her the very best that life has to offer. It is also my hope that Melanie's story will serve as a reminder that increasing student engagement is essential to improving educational outcomes.

Kristen Bonanno-Sotiropoulos

To Chad Mazza—your faith in my talents as a special educator and an educational leader have been unwavering over the years. Through your guidance, patience, and trust, I have achieved many professional and personal goals. I can't thank you enough for the encouragement, faith, and friendship.

Jennifer Smolinski

To Chad, whose parents told him he would never be successful—so he gave up; to Hanna, my daughter, who always tells me never to give up; to my son Ben, who has yet to give up; and to my son Ryan, who is too young to know what it is to give up.

Contents

Acknowledgments	ix
Introduction	1
1 Leveraging School Law to Promote School Improvement	7
2 Effective Leadership: Orchestrating the Band	19
3 Fostering Collaboration with Teachers' Unions	31
4 Effective Professional Development Opportunities	41
5 Promoting Academic Rigor in the Classroom Using Evidence-Based Practices	49
6 Innovative Instruction and Assessment Practices to Advance Student Outcomes	57
7 Response to Intervention as a Pathway to Student Success	69
8 Early Childhood and Special Populations: Considerations That Impact Learning	75
9 The Importance of Social-Emotional Learning in Fostering Positive Outcomes	85
10 Engaging Families in Positive Educational Outcomes	95
11 Promoting Community Partnerships	105
References	117
About the Authors	133

Acknowledgments

This book would not be complete without a heartfelt "thank you" to Sue Clark. She willingly gave her time and talents to editing this tome, which clearly made it stronger.

Introduction

Achieving Results: Maximizing Student Success in the Schoolhouse is designed to be a valuable resource for all educators, classroom teachers, school administrators, higher education faculty, preservice teachers, and parents who seek to gain a better understanding of how to attain positive outcomes within the classroom. Readers will benefit from the extensive research provided on a wide range of relevant topics, coupled with the focus on how to apply this knowledge to school improvement.

Our motivation for writing this book stems from several concerns:

- *Our deep commitment to ensuring that all students experience meaningful academic and social-emotional development so that they can become contributing members of a democratic society;*
- *Our belief that creating positive academic and personal gains requires many constituencies and approaches, not the least of which is the active engagement of students themselves;*
- *Our concern that only 37 percent of twelfth graders are proficient in reading, 25 percent are proficient in math, and 22 percent are proficient in science when they graduate (DeSilver, 2017);*
- *Our awareness, through experience and a careful examination of relevant research, that students can achieve academic proficiency through well-developed and supported educational programming; and*
- *Our knowledge that in order for students to achieve maximum results, there needs to be a concerted effort to identify and support diversity in its many forms.*

Today's schools are comprised of students who represent disparate populations. Students with disabilities, with limited English proficiency, from diverse backgrounds, or from disadvantaged homes present a unique set of needs, challenges, and dynamics. This presents the need for well-prepared educators, successful inclusive environments, strong relationships, and synergy between all stakeholders to harness the collective contributions of the full school community and leverage the potency of the school experience.

An important step to ensure that maximum preparedness occurs for educators, at all levels, is to become knowledgeable in identifying the needs of students, creating positive and safe learning environments, and negotiating progressive partnerships. Within the pages of this book are insights and suggestions to assist them with establishing these well-rounded educational experiences.

While lifelong educators and supporters of public schools, the authors appreciate the need to take stock of the current challenges facing our administrators, teachers, and students in our schools as a starting point in this discussion. We have highlighted challenges associated with academic achievement while recognizing that there are mounting and compelling social-emotional needs in schools associated with growing childhood mental health issues, social isolation, and even targeted bullying (Allen-Heath, Smith, & Young, 2017; Darling-Hammond, Wilhoit, & Pittenger, 2014; World Health Organization, 2017).

Alarming statistical data paints a dismal landscape concerning academic achievement in America's public schools. The Programme for International Student Assessment (PISA) shows that the United States ranks 38th in math and 24th in science, out of 71. Further, the Organization for Economic Cooperation and Development (OECD) identifies the United States as 30th in math, 17th in reading, and 19th in science, out of only 35 participating countries (DeSilver, 2017; OECD, 2012). This data is disturbing and supports the critical need to change the face of education as we know it today. If the United States wants to be successful in competing worldwide, the time is now to transform what education means for all of us.

The National Assessment of Educational Progress (NAEP) shows similar results. The most current data from 2015 indicates the average math scores for both fourth and eighth graders decreased from 2013; while in reading, fourth grade scores flatlined and eighth grade reading scores fell during that same time frame (The Nation's Report Card, n.d.). Reading proficiency for twelfth graders was equally dismal, with results showing that only 37 percent were proficient in reading at the time of the 2015 assessment (The Nation's Report Card, n.d.; DeSilver, 2017).

With regard to science, NAEP testing revealed that in 2015 only 38 percent of fourth graders, 34 percent of eighth graders, and 22 percent of twelfth graders were proficient (DeSilver, 2017; The Nation's Report Card, n.d.). The steady decline in scores as students advance through school is glaringly

Introduction 3

obvious and warrants a deeper examination into why this is happening at such an alarming rate, and how we, as concerned educators and parents, can find solutions to benefit student outcomes.

According to a 2012 report from the Organization for Economic Cooperation and Development, Massachusetts is a strong-performing state in comparison to Shanghai, China. OECD (2012) also points out that the United States tends to spend much more per student compared to other countries; however, this has not translated into better performance for our students. One could surmise, perhaps, that it is not the money the United States is spending, but rather how it is being spent differently than other countries with similar funding, that is the issue.

Looking at math specifically, students in the United States show extreme weaknesses in tasks involving higher cognitive demands "such as taking real-world situations [and] translating them into mathematical terms" (OECD, 2012, p. 2). It has been suggested that implementation of the Common Core Standards will improve weaknesses found in deep thinking; however, teachers must be consistent in the delivery of content and instructional strategies that support student learning. To do this, teacher preparation programs must be well-rounded, while school districts need to provide consistent professional development opportunities that target teaching weaknesses. Professional development should be offered to all educators and span the career continuum. This change begins with focused, in-depth, and well-rounded teacher preparation programs, and it should continue within school districts throughout the career of the teacher.

Ensuring that students are proficient in writing is critical to passing high-stakes testing, a requirement for graduation, qualifying for acceptance to postsecondary schools, and being career ready (Flanagan & Bouck, 2015; Troia & Olinghouse, 2013). Sadly, it is estimated that only 27 percent of students in grades eight and twelve are proficient or higher in writing, and an alarming 74 percent are below the proficiency level (Harris & Graham, 2013; National Center for Education Statistics, 2012). It is imperative to improve writing outcomes if the United States is to move the pendulum in the right direction.

Other startling statistics of concern are the dropout rates in the United States. It is estimated that 1.2 million students drop out of school in the United States each year, which amounts to 7,000 per day (DoSomething.Org, n.d.). According to the National Center for Education Statistics (2017), approximately 6 percent of all high school students have dropped out. A deeper dive into this statistic reveals that there are higher percentages of males than females who drop out, and that certain ethnic groups tend to have higher dropout rates (NCES, 2017; Diament, 2016; DoSomething.Org, n.d.).

4   *Introduction*

These rates are worrisome, as these are the same individuals who are more likely to experience job insecurity, higher rates of crime, alcohol and substance abuse, failed marriages, and continued financial support through state and federal programs (Diament, 2016). The Nation's Report Card (n.d.) pointed out that the dropout rate had decreased by 3 percent between 1990 and 2010, giving reason for optimism; however, more must be done to combat this issue.

As a result of this distressing information on the challenges facing our educators, this book was written to highlight approaches and strategies that have been found to improve student outcomes. Administrative factors, educational policy and law, collaborating with teachers' unions, and fostering partnerships with parents and community organizations all play a role in the bigger picture of improving student outcomes. More specific to classroom instruction, this book would not be complete without a discussion on the importance of implementation of evidence-based teaching practices, meaningful professional development, and considerations for early childhood and special populations of students, all of which have been found to play a role in achieving results.

The overarching theme, however, is that to become a high-functioning classroom or school, educators must be charged with continued improvement and will need to take active steps to address all of these areas simultaneously. To assist the reader, the authors have organized the book into the aforementioned chapter topics that hold the most promise in improving educational outcomes. Within each chapter, the relevant research and information is presented, and, to the extent practical, effective practices have been identified to support immediate implementation.

As you prepare to embark on the journey of reading this book, we encourage you to keep three things in mind: First, the authors appreciate the challenges associated with teaching, leading change in school organizations, and parenting school-aged children. We have more than fifty years of combined experience serving in the varying roles of teacher, principal, school psychologist, guidance counselor, director of student services, and school superintendent.

Second, the authors acknowledge that for sustained results to be possible, it takes the continuous effort and support of educators, the teachers' union, parents, policymakers, students, and the larger school community working in concert on a common impactful vision for their schools; however, it is understood that educators are the center of this equation and can marshal considerable support from school stakeholders when promoting meaningful, results-oriented school improvement.

Finally, we underscore that the work of improving classrooms and schools is time-consuming, requires sustained effort, and often occurs in

Introduction 5

small increments. While supporters of teachers, educational leaders, and our public institutions, the authors candidly recognize that the current education outcomes on a host of different measures create a clarion call for action. In short, we believe the American educational system can do better. To that end, we invite you through the proceeding pages to assist the next generation with achieving maximum results in the contemporary schoolhouse.

Chapter 1

Leveraging School Law to Promote School Improvement

School law is important in enhancing the quality of education, in that it drives the creation of policies that foster equal access to education and student success. Creating policies can be challenging, and it is imperative that administrators and teachers have a broad understanding of educational law and know the rights, privileges, and responsibilities that are associated with teaching.

Laws such as the Every Student Succeeds Act (ESSA) and Title I of the Elementary and Secondary Education Act (ESEA) have had a profound impact on the educational field (Klein, 2015). For example, part of the new ESSA (2015) required states to include nonacademic factors into accountability measures. This requirement helped promote an expanded vision of school success that extends beyond traditional measures such as standardized-test scores (Blad, 2016). Including measures to track school success, such as student engagement and access to advanced coursework, could provide schools with a more distinct and comprehensive view of student success and equity (Blad, 2016).

Title I grants for disadvantaged students are the foundation of the ESEA and speak to the hindrances that affect student learning and achievement, especially the impact of poverty on resources to public schools in underserved communities (National School Boards Association, 2015). Title I funds are utilized to support instructional strategies and methods that best meet local school needs to improve the overall instructional program, leading to an increased opportunity for all children to succeed in school (National School Board Association, 2015).

8   *Chapter 1*

SCHOOL ACCOUNTABILITY UNDER THE
EVERY STUDENT SUCCEEDS ACT

The new 2015 federal Every Student Succeeds Act has created one of the most powerful tools states have to ensure that all students—regardless of race, family income, home language, or disability status—receive the equal education they need and deserve (Students Can't Wait, 2015). The enactment of ESSA also reduced the federal government's role in education-accountability decisions by eliminating a vast array of requirements set forth by the No Child Left Behind Act (NCLB) and allowed states greater freedom in designing their own accountability systems (ASCD, 2017).

ESSA (Klein, 2015) required that states establish student performance goals and hold schools accountable for student achievement. It included comprehensive measures of student performance in their accountability systems beyond test scores (ASCD, 2017). ESSA (2015) also eliminated NCLB's specific list of remedial actions and required school improvement strategies, instead allowing school districts to design and implement their own improvement plans for low-performing schools (ASCD, 2017).

Accountability Systems

Systems of accountability were enacted not only to measure student and school performance, but also to identify which schools were in need of support and methods to take prompt action to raise student achievement (Students Can't Wait, 2015a). Accountability systems are sets of policies and practices that a state uses to hold schools and districts responsible for raising student achievement, to set and communicate expectations, to hold schools to higher achievement standards for all students, and to ensure there is progress for those students who are behind. Systems should be designed to create several achievable and reasonable priorities that focus on student success and improving student outcomes (Students Can't Wait, 2015b).

More specifically, accountability systems are comprised of two interconnected parts: a way to signal how well schools are doing, such as school rankings and ratings, and the actions that must occur from those ratings, such as recognition for high-performing schools and resources, supports, and interventions for struggling schools (Students Can't Wait, 2015).

While accountability systems cannot raise student achievement or reduce inequities in learning opportunities, they can serve several essential functions. Holding districts and schools accountable sets clear expectations that they must raise the achievement bar for all students, not just a particular subset of students. Assessment results can be used to ensure that there is clear communication on whether schools are indeed meeting those expectations for students overall and for each particular group of students served in the district (Students Can't Wait, 2015a).

Assessment measures can also be used to determine whether students have the knowledge and capability of meeting the new, rigorous academic standards and assessments for college readiness. Schools that meet or exceed expectations and standards for all groups of students should be celebrated, while schools that are struggling to attain their goals should be given additional resources and support in a prompt and timely manner to help them improve (Students Can't Wait, 2015).

School Ratings

Under ESSA (2015), states must develop an accountability system that includes performance goals on state assessments, at least one other valid and reliable indicator that can include student growth, and at least one indicator of school quality or student success that allows for meaningful differentiation, such as student engagement or school climate (Students Can't Wait, 2015b; National Association of School Psychologists, 2016; The Education Trust, 2014). States must then assign ratings to schools based on how they perform against these goals, as well as another academic indicator for elementary and middle schools, and an additional indicator of school quality for all schools (Students Can't Wait, 2015).

It is imperative that accountability systems are well designed so that educational disparities are apparent. Poorly designed systems will create a disservice to education by actually hiding student achievement gaps in opportunity and allowing underperformance to be ignored (Students Can't Wait, 2015). A limited number of high-quality indicators, which provide critical information on how schools serve their students, must be included in a school's rating system (Students Can't Wait, 2015).

ESSA (2015) requirements provide important protections for underserved student groups, in that school ratings must be based on how schools are performing for all groups of students, making it more difficult for schools to hide the failure to support certain groups behind the achievement of other students (ESSA, 2015; Students Can't Wait, 2015; The Education Trust, 2014). ESSA does leave the decision on what to measure, how to define underperformance, and how to support low-performing schools up to individual states. Although states are under pressure to make their schools look good, educational advocates must push states to measure what matters most (ESSA, 2015; Students Can't Wait, 2015).

When designing accountability systems, state educational leaders will need to answer questions such as: Which indicators should be used to measure school performance? How should the chosen indicators be combined into the formation of a school rating? and, How will it be ensured that ratings are meaningful and accurately reflect how schools are performing for all groups of students? (Students Can't Wait, 2015a).

ESSA (2015) allows states not only to decide what components make up accountability systems, but also to decide how much weight each component holds, although academic factors must be given more weight (ASCD, 2017; National Association of School Psychologists, 2016; The Education Trust, 2014). If school climate and student access to advanced coursework were measured, for example, results on state tests, English learner proficiency rates, and graduation rates would have to be given greater weight (ASCD, 2017).

The requirement that schools use one nonacademic indicator in accountability measures recognizes that test scores alone should not be used to measure student achievement, educator effectiveness, or school success (ESSA, 2015; ASCD, 2017). ESSA (2015) provides specific examples of possible measures such as school climate and safety, student or educator engagement, access to advanced coursework, and postsecondary readiness, but it does not specify which indicators schools must choose (ASCD, 2017).

School ranking criteria must, at a minimum, include indicators that are focused on students and reflect how schools are serving the individual needs of the students, particularly those of low-income families and students with disabilities (Students Can't Wait, 2015). To help ensure school ratings reflect how schools are meeting the needs of all student groups, ESSA (2015) requires all indicators to be disaggregated by student group. States must also align indicators with the ultimate goal of preparing all students for college readiness and success in higher education or in a meaningful career (Students Can't Wait, 2015).

Rating schools is beneficial, in that the ratings communicate expectations for preparing all groups of students for academic and professional endeavors after secondary school completion, how schools are performing against these expectations, and that improvement may be needed when outcomes for any group of students do not consistently meet expectations (Students Can't Wait, 2015).

School Improvement

According to ESSA (2015), every three years, states must use data from their accountability process to identify schools in need of support and improvement. This list should include schools that are very low-performing (in the bottom 5 percent) for all students, have graduation rates less than 67 percent, are consistently underperforming for any group of students, and are very low-performing (in the bottom 5 percent) for one or more groups of students (ASCD, 2017; Students Can't Wait, 2015; National Association of School Psychologists, 2016).

When schools have been identified as needing improvement, ESSA (2015) requires districts to conduct a needs assessment and work with schools, educators, and families to develop and implement evidence-based strategies and plans for improvement, and identify and address resource inequities such as inadequate funding and staffing ratios (ASCD, 2017; Students Can't Wait, 2015b; National Association of School Psychologists, 2016).

It is essential that states establish a coherent improvement process that supports school leaders in their improvement efforts. The school improvement process should start with a needs assessment to understand the underlying causes of school underperformance (Students Can't Wait, 2015b). Next, schools should work with district administrators to develop coherent strategies to address the challenges that were identified in the school's needs assessment.

A single improvement plan should be created that specifies what action will be taken, by whom, and what support and resources are necessary in carrying out those actions (Students Can't Wait, 2015). Benchmarks should also be established for yearly expected improvement (Students Can't Wait, 2015b). Once the strategies from the improvement plan are implemented in the school, districts should monitor the progress of school improvement using the previously established benchmarks. If schools do not improve within a reasonable amount of time, districts should require and support any additional action (Students Can't Wait, 2015).

Under ESSA (2015), although school improvement decisions are made by the states and districts, specific types of schools are required to take action if they are in need of improvement (Students Can't Wait, 2015b). The lowest-performing schools, which are those in the bottom 5 percent, and high schools with low graduation rates must work in conjunction with districts to propose improvement plans that specifically identify resource inequities to the state. The state then determines the level of performance that schools must reach before they are no longer identified as a school in need (exit criteria). Schools have four years to meet the state-set criteria before the state will require that they take additional action (Schools Can't Wait, 2015b).

Those schools where one or more groups of students are consistently underperforming must submit an improvement plan to the district and improve within a determined number of years before additional action is required (Students Can't Wait, 2015b). Schools that have one or more groups of students whose performance places them in the bottom 5 percent of Title I schools must also submit an improvement plan, including any resource inequities. The state must set exit criteria for these schools, and if the criteria are not met in a specified number of years, the state must treat the school as it would the lowest-performing schools (Students Can't Wait, 2015b).

Out of the $13 billion in general Title I funds, approximately $1 billion is set aside specifically for school improvement. ESSA (2015) specifies that when school improvement funds are distributed, priority should be given to districts that serve the most schools in need of support and improvement, demonstrate the greatest need, and show the strongest commitment to improving student achievement and student outcomes (Students Can't Wait, 2015).

TITLE I OF THE ELEMENTARY AND SECONDARY EDUCATION ACT

Title I of the Elementary and Secondary Education Act of 1965 (ESEA), as amended by the No Child Left Behind Act (NCLB), is the largest U.S. government educational program assisting disadvantaged children (National Center for Education Statistics [NCES], 2016). Title I provides funding to schools to improve learning for students at risk of educational failure, including those students who are low-achieving children in poverty-stricken schools, children with disabilities, and children and parents who are in need of family-literacy services (NCES, 2016; U.S. Department of Education, 2015).

Funding

Funds allocated under Title I are intended to provide additional and/or targeted instruction and support to disadvantaged children as a way to master challenging school programs and meet state standards in core academic subjects (U.S. Department of Education, 2015; Lexia, 2016). ESEA (1965) does not stipulate how Title I funds are to be spent and is meant to provide flexibility to state and local educational agencies to spend as they deem appropriate (NCES, 2016; NASP, 2016; Lexia, 2016). Typically, funds are used to support extended-day kindergarten programs, special after-school and summer programs that extend and reinforce regular school curriculum, and other services that accelerate academic progress (NCES, 2016; U.S. Department of Education, 2015).

The U.S. Department of Education is responsible for the allocation of Title I funds to local education agencies (LEAs), states, U.S. territories, and other educational agencies, to enable elementary and secondary schools to create and sustain programs that will improve the educational opportunities of low-income and disadvantaged children (NCES, 2016). Funds are awarded based on the number of children eligible for Title I support and the per-pupil cost of education, and they are given out in the form of basic grants, concentration grants, targeted grants, and education finance incentive grants (NCES, 2016; U.S. Department of Education, 2015).

Basic grants are the primary vehicle for Title I funding, and they accounted for approximately $6.5 billion of Title I funds distributed in the fiscal year of 2015 (FY 2015) (NCES, 2016). Concentration grants provide additional funds to LEAs with large populations of low-income and disadvantaged children, and they accounted for approximately $1.3 billion in FY 2015 (NCES 2016).

Targeted grants provide additional funds according to a weighting system, which ensures that the greatest proportion of funding is distributed to LEAs with the greatest number of low-income and disadvantaged children, and they constituted approximately $3.3 billion of allocations in FY 2015 (NCES, 2016). Lastly, education finance incentive grants provide LEAs with additional funding for low-income and disadvantaged children depending on measures of state equity and effort in funding public education, and they accounted for approximately $3.3 billion in FY 2015 (NCES, 2016).

Specialized Instructional Support

ESSA affords schools considerable opportunities to increase access to comprehensive school services and to advance the role of support specialists to help improve student success and school outcomes (National Association of School Psychologists [NASP], 2016). States and LEAs are required to engage in meaningful consultation with appropriate specialized instructional support personnel when designing state and local Title I plans to improve student outcomes and school success (NASP, 2016)

Specialized instructional support personnel can include school counselors, social workers, and psychologists, and any other qualified professional, such as a school nurse, speech-language pathologist, or school librarian, who is involved in providing assessment, diagnosis, counseling, educational, therapeutic, and other necessary services (NASP, 2016). In schools managing targeted assistance programs, strategies must demonstrate how specialized instructional support personnel will assist in identifying and intervening with those students at greatest risk of failure (NASP, 2016).

Although states must report school climate, bullying, and harassment data every year and the methods they will undertake to address these issues, ESSA (2015) affords states flexibility in determining which specific methods they will utilize to make improvements. States may use Title I funds to implement layered systems of support to address the academic, social-emotional, behavioral, and mental health needs of all students; improve the quality and effectiveness of school community partnerships; and offer professional development for all relevant school personnel, including instructional support specialists (NASP, 2016; Lexia, 2016).

14   *Chapter 1*

Title I Programs

Title I schools with a 40 percent population of low-income students may use Title I funds to implement and conduct a "schoolwide program" meant to advance the instructional program for the entire school (NASP, 2016; U.S. Department of Education, 2015; Lexia, 2016). Title I schools with less than a 40 percent population of low-income students, or that choose not to implement a schoolwide program, may offer a "targeted assistance program" (NASP, 2016; U.S. Department of Education, 2015; Lexia, 2016).

In this type of program, schools identify students who are failing, or who are most at risk of failing, to meet the state's prescribed academic achievement standards. Instructional programs are then designed to meet the needs of the identified students (NASP, 2016). Schoolwide and targeted assistance programs must employ instructional strategies tethered in scientifically based research and implement family engagement activities (NASP, 2016; Lexia, 2016).

LEAs are also required to provide services for eligible private school students (NASP, 2016; U.S. Department of Education, 2015). In particular, LEAs are required to provide eligible children, teachers, and families in private elementary and secondary schools with Title I services or other benefits equal to those provided to eligible public school children, their teachers, and their families (NASP, 2016; U.S. Department of Education, 2015).

Title I Students

With more focus on attaining levels of proficiency on state achievement tests, and the use of Title I funds to assist students in meeting academic goals, it is imperative that educators develop an understanding of the unique needs of Title I students in order to maximize student success (Lexia, 2016). Students requiring additional support under Title I are typically from low-income families and are often referred to as "students in poverty," they are students of low socioeconomic status, and they are students who are eligible for free or reduced-cost school lunches (Lexia, 2016).

The unique challenges these students encounter at home and in school often make it difficult at best, if not entirely impossible, to focus on academic achievement and personal success in school. Factors such as inadequate food and shelter and an unpredictable, unsafe living environment not only significantly impact a student's overall physical and emotional health, but they also affect academic and cognitive performance, as well as emotional engagement and in-school behavior (Lexia, 2016).

Research has shown that there are specific things that schools and teachers can do that will help Title I students succeed (Lexia, 2016). It is essential that school administrators and teachers devote time to understanding the issues that low-income students and families are dealing with and treat them with respect (Lexia, 2016). Teachers may provide differentiated and personalized instruction to address students' individual needs in ways that promote student success (Lexia, 2016). Universal design methods, including various teaching methods and choice of materials, can also be explored to help motivate students and allow frequent opportunities for success (Lexia, 2016).

SCHOOL RANKING OUTSIDE THE UNITED STATES AND MOVING FORWARD

Through an international lens, United States K–12 schools are neither excellent nor equal to their international counterparts (Stewart, 2012). For quite some time, countries around the world have been expanding education to maximize success, to promote individual health and well-being, and to reduce poverty, leaving the United States in a position where it is behind in not only the quantity of education, but also the quality of education (Stewart, 2012).

Recently released data from international math and science assessments indicates that U.S. students continue to rank in the middle when compared to other countries and may even be behind other advanced industrial nations (Desilver, 2017). The most recent cross-national test results, from 2015, placed the United States 38th out of 71 countries in math and 24th in science (Desilver, 2017).

Several countries have demonstrated effective, successful strategies that the United States may want to consider. Singapore's vision of education has strong ties to economic development and social cohesion (Stewart, 2012). While this connection may be harder to obtain in the United States, educational leaders could develop a forward-facing global focus on the development of education by fostering stronger collaboration among educators, businesses, families, and communities (Stewart, 2012).

Canadian schools are very similar to U.S. schools, in that they collaborate with unions and other stakeholders, focus on instructional content, and promote the development of effective teachers through various methods of professional development and support (Stewart, 2012). In alignment with Canada's strategies, the United States should continue to develop and maintain collaborative relationships with key stakeholders in education, such as teachers' unions, families, and institutions of higher education, to bring about policy change and reform (Stewart, 2012).

The United States has only recently begun to emulate the visions and strategies held in Asian countries. China's long-term vision for education, coherent systems for teacher development, and strong cultural commitment to education places it among the top-performing countries in the world (Stewart, 2012). Focus in the United States should continue to be placed on supporting teachers through various modes of professional development, including coaching and mentoring, to improve and enhance classroom instructional skills and curricula (Stewart, 2012).

To be on par with world-education and world-class content standards, the United States might consider revising curricula standards to cover a smaller number of topics in greater depth, enabling students to thoroughly learn a topic before moving on to the more difficult topics. Educational administrators should also move toward universal standards of education and away from the varying standards found across the United States (Stewart, 2012).

FINAL THOUGHTS

Not only does the ESSA reduce government power over the accountability of U.S. schools, it gives direct power to the states to ensure that every single student, regardless of race, income, or disability status, receives an equal education. School districts are handed the control to design accountability systems that measure school success and implement improvement plans for low-performing schools. While accountability systems cannot raise student achievement or reduce inequities, they hold educational leaders accountable and responsible for setting clear expectations of what is needed to increase achievement and student success for all students, not just a select group.

Accountability processes identify schools in need of support and improvement, and this includes schools that are very low-performing, have graduation rates less than 67 percent, are consistently underperforming, and have very low-performing students. Under these circumstances, districts must conduct a needs assessment and develop and implement evidence-based strategies and plans for improvement.

Title I is the largest government educational program that assists disadvantaged children in underperforming schools by providing funding to improve learning for students at risk of educational failure. With a greater focus on attaining levels of proficiency on state achievement tests and increased rates of student success, it is imperative that educators develop an understanding of the unique needs of Title I students in order to maximize student success.

Leveraging School Law to Promote School Improvement

POINTS TO REMEMBER

- Assessment measures are used to determine if student knowledge is sufficient to meet the new, rigorous academic standards and assessments for college readiness. The requirement that schools use one nonacademic indicator in assessment measures recognizes that test scores alone are not significant of student achievement, educator effectiveness, or school success.
- School ranking criteria must use indicators that focus on how the individual needs of all students are being met. To ensure that school ratings reflect how schools meet the needs of all student groups, assessment indicators must be disaggregated by student group.
- Schools identified as needing improvement must take action to make improvements. These schools include the lowest-performing schools, schools in which one or more groups of students are consistently underperforming, and schools that have one or more groups of students whose performance places them in the bottom 5 percent of Title I schools.
- Funds allocated under Title I provide support to disadvantaged children to meet the standards set by challenging school programs and by states in core academic subjects. States may use Title I funds to develop schoolwide programs to advance the instruction for the entire school or develop targeted assistance programs to meet the needs of students who are most at risk of failing.
- Children, teachers, and families in private elementary and secondary schools are eligible for the same Title I services as those students enrolled in public school.
- U.S. P-12 schools are neither excellent nor equal to their international counterparts and are actually behind in not only the quantity of education, but also the quality of education.

Chapter 2

Effective Leadership: Orchestrating the Band

Much like the conductor of a band or orchestra leads the different ensembles to work together in harmony to produce beautiful music, similar methods happen within our schools every day. The principal, also known as the instructional leader, works with all stakeholders to ensure that everyone works together, supporting one another through collaboration in order to complement the climate of the school, which supports student achievement.

The role of the principal has evolved over the years. Previously, the role of the school principal was more of an authoritative type, engaging in managerial tasks and commanding responsibilities, with a focus on organizing, planning, directing, and controlling. The modern-day principal, on the other hand, is a leader, one who influences and inspires others to succeed through the skills within management (Stein, 2016). True leaders empower individuals to facilitate change and support the vision and mission of the school (Toor, 2011).

Today's school leaders need to know how to build and maintain positive working relationships with all stakeholders, in conjunction with leading school improvement efforts (Estrella-Henderson & Jessop, 2015). Improved student achievement, however, is the most important outcome expected of the instructional leader (Brown, 2016).

LEADERSHIP VERSUS MANAGEMENT

School leadership has a direct correlation on school culture, student achievement, and school performance (Stein, 2016). Public schools require good leaders rather than business managers. Effective leadership, in addition to classroom instruction, directly influences student learning outcomes

(Stein, 2016). There continues to be a disconnect for many principals, that of how to be more of a leader than a manager. As a result, research has shown, American public schools are failing (Stein, 2016).

Successful leaders understand the complex nature of what motivates individuals and the beneficial characteristics of collaborative relationships (Stein, 2016). According to Toor (2011), leadership encompasses both change and sustainability; however, unlike management, it uses relationships to gain authority. Finally, leadership empowers individuals to facilitate change and support the vision and mission of the school (Toor, 2011).

Currently, views on leadership in education have moved from a hierarchical form to more of a distributive leadership style. Schools are now embracing, at an increased rate, leadership that embraces collegiality and collaboration (Stein, 2016). Through distributive leadership, schools are empowering participatory decision-making and teacher leadership in order to make vast improvements from the inside (Stein, 2016). Leadership should center around bringing people together for a common good through supported collaboration.

In a 2016 study by Stein, it was stated that leadership positions should be reserved for individuals who believe in collaboration and teamwork and who possess the active listening skills needed to keep an open mind (Stein, 2016). When it comes to supporting teachers, there are certain tasks that successful leaders embrace. The first is to communicate a clear and realistic mission statement. The mission statement establishes the priorities set forth to support the success of the school. It is important that all stakeholders, including teachers, students, and families, understand the mission (Stein, 2016).

An effective leader is an agent of change who believes in transparency, support, and shared decision-making. Empowering others, leaders must do a superior job of inspiring their faculty to contribute in the decision-making process. High visibility is a critical skill of effective leaders and although this requires time, the benefits are great. Leaders who are visible throughout the school environment improve staff morale and contribute to a positive school culture. Setting the right example provides a model for the rest of the school community. Leaders with a strong work ethic, a positive attitude, and a high level of integrity serve to promote the same in their schools (Stein, 2016).

THE PRINCIPAL AS INSTRUCTIONAL LEADER

Current views of instructional leadership believe that there are three critical areas that principals need to focus on in order to provide positive instructional guidance: defining the school's mission, managing instructional programs, and encouraging a positive learning environment (Mitchell, Kensler, & Tschannen-Moran, 2015).

In a 2015 study conducted by Mitchell et al., significant findings revealed the importance of "creating a climate of academic press to foster student achievement" (p. 244). "Academic press," according to the authors, refers to the focus on academic achievement through the setting of high expectations for all students. The way to attain this type of climate is through the instructional leadership of the principal (Mitchell et al., 2015).

In a review of the literature, five themes of successful school principals were revealed. The five themes include the qualities of effective leadership, the establishment of the school's vision and goals, positively impacting the climate and culture of the school, the personal traits and characteristics of the school leader, and finally, the influence that school leadership has on student achievement (Brown, 2016; Mitchell et al., 2015).

School Leaders as Instructional Coaches

Research has suggested that instructional leadership coaching is highly effective at increasing student achievement (Estrella-Henderson & Jessop, 2015). The research identified the following key practices of instructional leadership coaches that are critical to increasing student success:

- A caring attitude: Instructional leadership coaches who care deeply display support and fairness when working with all staff and students;
- Honesty and openness: This is met through shared decision-making, honoring agreements, and demonstrating transparency;
- Competence and reliability: This is displayed through conflict resolution, showing flexibility, problem-solving skills, consistency, and being committed to school improvement efforts; and
- Encouraging a climate of trust: This is equally important for attracting the support of all stakeholders (Estrella-Henderson & Jessop, 2015).

Building the Leadership Capacity in Others

Boren (2017) examined two approaches to synergistic school leadership: building team capacity and building team leader capacity. According to Boren (2017), these approaches are the best ways to improve student learning. Investing time and resources in increasing the learning of teachers ensures loyalty and hard work. Schools need principals, as well as instructional leaders, who are capable of creating communities of practice focused on best strategies for teaching and learning (Estrella-Henderson & Jessop, 2015).

The first approach focuses on building the capacity of teachers to work together collaboratively. Teachers who are allowed the time, resources, and guidance to engage as an instructional team are then able to increase their learning and effectiveness within the classroom, which directly impacts student achievement (Boren, 2017; Carroll, Fulton, & Doerr, 2010).

When encouraging teachers to work together in teams, it is imperative that there are supports in place that guide the teamwork process. Many times, teachers get together in collaborative efforts and simply have no direction or idea of what they should be doing. Principals can encourage effective teamwork through modeling, coaching, and simply being present; however, being present can introduce time constraints and an overreliance on the principal and therefore this should be used with caution (Boren, 2017).

The second approach, building team leader capacity, supports the development of an instructional team leader. Team leaders are viewed as the key link between administration and faculty (Boren, 2017). If principals invest a small amount of time in building the expertise of and supporting the leadership development in their team leaders, this will help to create better environments for teaching and learning. Team leaders can then be used to free up the principal's time to participate in other leadership opportunities.

Principals can support their instructional team leaders through the implementation of monthly leadership team meetings. During leadership team meetings, members engage in collaboration centered around how to lead a team at each grade level, in each content area, or in the student population. As a result, team leaders increase their efficiency while leading their individual teams (Boren, 2017).

ADMINISTRATIVE FACTORS TO CREATING AND MAINTAINING INCLUSIVE SCHOOLS

There has been an increase in students with disabilities included in mainstream classrooms. This, combined with high standards and accountability systems, makes the demand for inclusive schools a priority. Inclusive learning environments provide opportunities for individuals with disabilities to engage and connect with peers, access rich academic instruction, and experience full access to the learning community (Theoharis & Causton, 2014). Creating such inclusive schools begins with exceptional leadership.

To establish successful inclusive schools, school leaders must employ several critical strategies, to include: setting a vision, developing implementation plans, using staff in systematic ways through inclusive delivery services, establishing and supporting collaborative teams to support student needs, providing ongoing and meaningful learning opportunities for staff, monitoring and adjusting service delivery options, and creating and maintaining a climate of belonging for both students and staff (Theoharis & Causton, 2014). According to Theoharis and Causton (2014), these strategies can be implemented in six steps.

The first step, setting a vision for the school, enables all stakeholders to understand what the school's goal actually is. A vision statement endorses the beliefs of the school and provides direction in relation to supporting best practices in teaching and learning, including the goal of education (Gabriel & Farmer, 2009). When setting a vision for an inclusive school, three areas should be addressed: the structure of the school, meeting the needs of all students in general education settings, and the school climate (Theoharis & Causton, 2014).

Step two involves creating service delivery maps. To begin, school personnel must examine the current way in which students are serviced and the availability of resources. The examination process should conclude with a map, or a visual representation, of the current practices within the school (Theoharis & Causton, 2014).

The third step in the process involves aligning school structures. During this process, schools look at rearranging personnel to create teams that can support the needs of all students. Throughout this step, administrators create new inclusive service delivery maps that may include rearranging staff in order to create balanced and heterogeneous classrooms (Theoharis & Causton, 2014).

Creating instructional teams is the fourth step in the process, and it has two phases. It begins by ensuring that each instructional team is made up of a general education teacher, a special education teacher, an ELL teacher, and paraprofessionals. The second phase focuses on establishing classrooms that are aligned with the school's natural proportion of students. By using the school's natural proportion as a guide, the ability to create classrooms that are balanced, heterogeneous, and with a mix of abilities is strengthened (Theoharis & Causton, 2014).

Step five provides meaningful professional development opportunities to teachers and other educators in order to impact classroom practices. Professional development plans should be created in advance, aligned with instructional practices, and established for teachers, administrators, and paraprofessionals. Meaningful professional development supports the effectiveness of all educators. It is recommended that professional development focus on such topics as differentiated instruction, collaborative strategies, evidence-based practices, and working with challenging behaviors (Theoharis & Causton, 2014).

The sixth component of the process is ongoing monitoring and adjustment of the reform plan. The monitoring occurs through feedback gathered from all stakeholders, including teachers, parents, and students. The final step in the reform process is creating and maintaining a climate of belonging. All stakeholders should be involved in building communities in the classrooms, the school, and the outside community (Theoharis & Causton, 2014).

STAFF MEETINGS: HOW ADMINISTRATORS CAN MAKE THEM MORE ENGAGING

Most teachers dread monthly staff meetings. Experience has proven that staff meetings are usually unengaging, uninteresting, and passive in nature. Johnson (2015) encourages the use of technology as a means of increasing active participation and opportunities for authentic discussion, and compares it to what teachers do every day in their classrooms to engage their students.

The three main reasons cited for incorporating technology into staff meetings, as well as professional development opportunities, include modeling the use of technology, creation of meaningful meetings, and the ability to go paperless. If technology is utilized by adults for adults, the opportunity to model high expectations, demonstrate appropriate usage, and provide instruction on various device techniques are bonus outcomes of said meetings (Johnson, 2015).

The use of technology can support the creation of meaningful meetings by engaging participants in interactive activities. Most staff meetings are presented through the use of a PowerPoint slideshow, from which the presenter typically reads. This creates a passive learning environment. Using technology engages staff members and brings everyone into the discussion.

Technology that includes response systems, cloud-based tools such as Google Docs, online tools such as Padlet (Renard, 2017), and web-based software such as Animoto (2017) provides the presenter with creative, collaborative options for engaging individuals as active participants (Johnson, 2015). Finally, through the incorporation of technology, schools are able to go completely paperless. Through the use of apps such as Google Docs, it is easy to share documents, collaboratively edit, and disperse with ease.

RECRUITING AND KEEPING HIGH-QUALITY TEACHERS

Under federal regulations, teachers are required to be highly qualified. When highly qualified teachers are in the classroom, student achievement can rise. When states can help districts organize the preparation, recruitment, and retention efforts of highly qualified teachers, it is easier to ensure that they are in every classroom (Williby, 2004). The equal distribution of teachers is an

Effective Leadership   25

ongoing problem within the United States. Large urban districts and poorer communities usually tend to have the greatest need for well-qualified teachers (Williby, 2004). In a 2011 study, 31 percent of teachers in these types of geographical regions had quit within the first five years (Savage, 2011). This rate is even higher within urban school districts—at an astounding 50 percent (Rizga, 2015).

Recruiting Efforts and Teacher Selection

Before a school can recruit and select teachers, important characteristics must be specified. Attitudes, behaviors, and skills are most notable in the selection process. When reviewing teacher candidates for positions, those characteristics should promote excellence in the classroom (Savage, 2011). Research identifies several mistakes that administrators make throughout the hiring process, such as narrowing the hiring criteria, failing to emphasize specific academic criteria, failure to fully assess a candidate's ability to interact positively with students, and not including all interested parties in the hiring process (Williby, 2004).

Once the job description has been developed to meet the needs of the school, the evaluation process starts. Having a team to conduct the evaluations is a critically important component of effective school leaders. When teams are engaged in the evaluation process, having a rating document is helpful at weeding individuals out and identifying those who will be brought in for an interview (Williby, 2004). When reviewing documents, it is important to evaluate the quality of written expression. Williby (2004) also suggests obtaining a copy of college transcripts to ascertain the caliber of the candidate.

Conducting interviews should encompass one to three individual interviews, and then a group interview. During the interview process, 70 percent of the questions should be competency-based and focus on instructional skills, professional knowledge, classroom behavior, and interpersonal skills (Williby, 2004).

Retaining High-Quality Teachers

Once school districts are fortunate enough to hire highly qualified teachers, the task becomes how to retain them. Statistical data shows that new teachers leave the teaching profession for various reasons, including large workloads, assignment to the most difficult students, teaching assignments not in their certification field, and limited interactions with mentor teachers (Rizga, 2015; Savage, 2011). There are several things that school administrators can do to ensure their efforts to retain staff succeed, one of which is the use of peer

26   *Chapter 2*

observations to increase new teacher performance. Peer observations are considered a form of professional development (Williby, 2004).

The creation and funding of high-quality induction programs provides the necessary supports for new teachers. An educator who participates in an induction program during the first three years of teaching is less likely to quit (Rizga, 2015). Induction programs include time and resources for peer observations, support groups, seminars, and mentoring. Induction programs, when effectively developed, have proven beneficial at reducing the teacher attrition rate from 50 percent to 15 percent (Williby, 2004; Rizga, 2015).

TEACHER EVALUATION

With the passing of the Every Student Succeeds Act of 2015 (ESSA), there has been a shift from the preceding law, No Child Left Behind (NCLB), on how school districts should support teacher improvement efforts. According to Rosen and Parise (2017), the vision of ESSA was to assist school districts in identifying teacher needs, through the teacher evaluation system, and support them with professional development opportunities aligned to their individual needs.

Teacher Evaluation and Professional Growth under the Every Student Succeeds Act

The Every Student Succeeds Act of 2015 (ESSA) has both suggestions and statements pertaining to both teacher evaluation and professional development efforts. First, ESSA clearly states that professional development must be embedded within a teacher's job, as part of the larger school and/or district improvement plan, and it must address the specific areas of weakness identified in a teacher's observation (Rosen & Parise, 2017). The vision set forth by ESSA embodies a cycle of professional development opportunities that support school improvement efforts.

ESSA, however, does not have statements specific to teacher evaluation, but rather suggestions. First, ESSA allows school districts to use Title II improvement funds to invest in teacher evaluation systems and professional development opportunities (Rosen & Parise, 2017). ESSA also suggests that school districts identify and create career ladders for teachers consisting of supports and resources to assist with moving up within the school district, such as in administrative positions (Rosen & Parise, 2017).

Rosen and Parise (2017) conducted a study that evaluated, through surveys, the promise of ESSA: teacher evaluation and professional development. The survey data suggested that there are discrepancies in the views

Effective Leadership 27

between principals and teachers. Differences in whether or not professional development activities were sufficient and meaningful, based upon the areas of weakness identified in the teacher evaluation. Statistical data revealed the following: Seventy-four percent of principals thought that a teacher's formal evaluation highly or moderately contributed to the specific professional development assignments, whereas only 36 percent of teachers agreed (Rosen & Parise, 2017).

Furthermore, only 56 percent of teachers said that after being observed they were provided with useful professional development suggestions (Rosen & Parise, 2017). In addition, 20 percent of teachers reported receiving *no* suggestions for professional development after being observed (Rosen & Parise, 2017).

A "large percentage" (the exact number was not provided) of principals felt unsupported when identifying professional development needs and resources meant to provide meaningful professional development opportunities for their teachers (Rosen & Parise, 2017). These findings suggest that there is a communication barrier between the administration and teachers. Principals need to be able to effectively and concretely offer feedback and opportunities for professional growth.

FINAL THOUGHTS

The most important role of the school principal is to improve student achievement outcomes (Brown, 2016). There are three critical focus areas for school principals. The first is defining the school's mission and vision. Second, they must oversee the effectiveness of the instructional programs. Encouraging and supporting positive learning environments, or fostering the school culture, is the third (Mitchell et al., 2015).

The literature has identified the differences between being a leader compared to being a manager. Management focuses on such tasks as organizing, planning, directing, and controlling, whereas leading involves influencing and inspiring others to succeed, using some managerial skills (Stein, 2016). Successful leaders acknowledge the complex nature of motivating individuals and the positive results that can occur as a result of collaborative relationships (Stein).

Although there are many theories as to what makes an effective school leader and what components are critical to raising student achievement, many researchers have similar ideas. Brown (2016) identified several factors that contribute to the effectiveness of school leaders: clearly establishing the school's mission and vision, creating and maintaining a positive school culture, and the personal character traits of the individuals themselves.

Similarly, Estrella-Henderson and Jessop (2015) established critical skills and practices of school administrators as instructional coaches. These practices include having a caring attitude; being honest, open, and transparent; displaying competence and reliability; and supporting a climate of trust.

School administrators need to create learning environments that ensure student success. There are many leadership components that factor into creating bountiful learning cultures. In order to ensure that all elements are met, school leaders should engage in the use of team building and team leaders to support leadership efforts. Boren (2017) offers two strategies for accomplishing this.

Building the capacity of school teams through investing in the learning of the teachers improves student outcomes. When administration supports the collaboration efforts of instructional teams through providing time and resources, classroom instruction improves, which directly affects student achievement (Boren, 2017).

As much as administrators would like to be part of the collaboration process during team time, this is often not possible given time restraints; therefore, the investment in creating and supporting instructional team leaders makes sense. By investing in time to grow the capacity of teachers who can then become instructional team leaders, the school administrator is creating a link between administration and staff (Boren, 2017).

Creating effective leadership to support the many tenets of inclusive schools is of utmost importance. With the diverse student populations becoming the norm, schools must be sufficiently prepared to address the various needs of students with disabilities, low socioeconomic status, and English language learners. Theoharis and Causton (2014) explain the strategies and the steps schools need to take in order to create successful inclusive schools.

These strategies include such things as setting a vision, developing service delivery plans using available staff and resources in strategic ways, consistent and meaningful professional development opportunities, monitoring and adjusting the implementation plan, and maintaining a climate of belonging for both students and staff (Theoharis & Causton, 2014).

POINTS TO REMEMBER

- School administrators must focus on three critical areas: creating and supporting the school's mission and vision, managing the instructional programs, and encouraging a positive learning culture.
- Schools are embracing collaborative decision-making as well as increased teacher leadership opportunities in order to make positive improvements in teaching and learning.

- Leadership, not management, centers around bringing people together for a common good through supported collaboration. Within the school environment, this means encouraging collegial planning and decision-making to increase student achievement.
- Improved student achievement is the most important outcome expected of the instructional leader. Positive student achievement can be obtained through recruiting and retaining highly qualified teachers, as well as identifying and supporting professional growth activities based on teacher evaluations.
- Creating and supporting the capacity of teachers to become instructional leaders is an important way to link administration and staff. School leaders who invest time in supporting the development of leadership skills in certain teachers have more opportunities to facilitate change.

Chapter 3

Fostering Collaboration with Teachers' Unions

Effective public schools are built on strong collaborative relationships between union leaders, administrators, and educators who seek to provide opportunities to identify problems, plan, make decisions, and integrate solutions (Anrig, 2014; Rubinstein & McCarthy, 2014). These strong relationships focus on teacher effectiveness and educational improvement to help students become more successful (Rubinstein & McCarthy, 2014).

High-quality, school-level, teacher-administrator partnerships foster widespread school-level collaboration and communication and serve to improve student performance, curriculum development, instructional practice, advising, and formal or informal mentoring (Rubinstein & McCarthy, 2014). Union-management partnerships are problem-focused and designed to use collaboration to create and implement solutions to the gaps in student achievement. The quality of formal partnerships between teachers' unions, administrators, and teachers can help improve student performance (Rubinstein & McCarthy, 2014).

THE DEBATE ON TEACHERS' UNIONS

Over the years, the debate over public school reform has created friction between teachers' unions, administrators, school boards, parents, and policymakers in public education and has led to disagreements on how the quality of teaching and learning for children can be improved (Rubinstein & McCarthy, 2014). Although the debate is continual, districts, schools, and union leaders have found that strong relationships between unions and management that facilitate collaboration and focus on teaching quality and educational improvement can lead to reform (Rubinstein & McCarthy, 2014).

32   *Chapter 3*

Together, the National Education Association (NEA) and the American Federation of Teachers (AFT) comprise the single most powerful force in American education policy (Antonucci, 2015). NEA membership is down more than 9 percent, while the AFT's steady membership is only maintained by affiliating with unions outside the educational field, not by recruiting new teachers (Antonucci, 2015). Many believe that teachers' unions are the biggest obstacle to educational reforms, in that they have long supported policies that protect inferior teachers at the expense of dedicated educators and students (Akash, 2014).

Teachers' unions have also been criticized for opposing the expansion of school choice, which would give low-income and minority students greater opportunity to attend successful schools and utilize educational options such as charter and private schools. By adding the option of school choice, unions would be adding accountability and opportunity that goes against their special interests (Antonucci, 2015).

As a result, positive public opinion of unions is in decline. Forty-three percent of the public believes unions have a negative effect on public schools, up from 31 percent in 2009 (Antonucci, 2015). At the same time, union membership is also in decline, as exemplified by the NEA's loss of 230,000 educators, which translates into 7 percent of their total membership (Antonucci, 2015). Teachers have reported that unions are no longer benefiting educators and their students and, in addition, that union efforts to expand outside education only serve to further alienate teachers (Antonucci, 2015).

With all the negativity, it may be difficult to see how unions can benefit students and schools in positive ways. Problem-focused union-management partnerships, however, help drive thinking about ways to increase student learning and are designed to use collaboration among educators to discover solutions to gaps in student achievement. As key stakeholders in the improvement process, they have tacit knowledge of the problems to be solved and are the first to implement solutions (Rubinstein & McCarthy, 2014).

Effective union-management teams also create a positive climate for teacher collaboration, leading to innovation and a strong infrastructure for problem-solving. Organizational structures can be established that allow for increased levels of teacher input in planning, problem-solving, and decision-making when positive alliances are formed (Rubinstein & McCarthy, 2014). Educational research has shown that greater levels of professional collaboration among teachers can be a successful tool in improving student achievement (Rubinstein & McCarthy, 2014).

Schools with positive union-management alliances have greater levels of communication and collaboration, which then leads to improved student performance (Rubinstein & McCarthy, 2014). When union leaders and management work together, teachers are more willing to engage in collaborative structures and processes (Rubinstein & McCarthy, 2014).

The quality of the partnership between teachers and administrators at the school level has a significant impact on educator collaboration and student achievement (Rubinstein & McCarthy, 2014). Research demonstrates that when unions, teachers, and school leaders have mutual respect and commitment to improved teaching and learning, positive student and school outcomes are inevitable (Rubinstein & McCarthy, 2014; Ravani, 2014).

Critics of teachers' unions claim there is no relationship between high levels of union membership and high levels of student achievement (Ravani, 2014). As of 2014, there were ten states where there was no collective bargaining by teachers, and if these critics are correct, these states should have demonstrated student achievement that ranks very high, or at least above the national average (Ravani, 2014). In reality, however, those states without binding teacher contracts are actually among the lowest academic performers in the nation, which suggests that it is in the best interest of schools and school districts to ensure a union-management partnership that is focused on working together for improved student outcomes (Ravani, 2014).

CREATING LONG-TERM PARTNERSHIPS

To create and support long-term partnerships, incentives should be provided for districts to establish union-management alliances that focus on the development of curriculum and instructional practice, teacher evaluation, professional development, and mentorship (Rubinstein & McCarthy, 2014). Technical and financial support is important as these teams strive to find innovative practices that influence quality teaching and student performance (Rubinstein & McCarthy, 2014).

To develop a school where a strong team approach can flourish, a joint committee should be organized and implemented to solve problems and make decisions important to the functioning of the school. Collaborative leadership team meetings must discuss substantive school issues, solve problems, and engage in site-based decision-making practices. Items to discuss might include textbook adoption, review of school schedules, guidance toward a quality hiring process, and other building-based items (Rubinstein & McCarthy, 2016).

In order for districts to establish and maintain union-management partnerships and use collaborative approaches, widespread support is needed from all stakeholders (Rubinstein & McCarthy, 2016). States should provide leadership training and skill development, learning networks, and mentorship for inexperienced teams, as well as ways for districts to build

34   *Chapter 3*

local capacity and facilitate organizational change and innovation (Rubinstein & McCarthy, 2016).

Massachusetts Education Partnership (MEP)

One of the two best-known teachers' unions, the American Federation of Teachers, collaborated with the Massachusetts Teachers Association, the Massachusetts Association of School Superintendents, the Massachusetts Association of School Committees, the Rennie Center, and representatives from three of the Commonwealth's most prominent research institutions to formally establish the Massachusetts Education Partnership (MEP) (Rennie Center, 2017).

The MEP works to improve student learning and success through collaborative labor management–community relations in school districts with the development and maintenance of more effective policies, structures, and practices. It is overseen by educators, leadership, and district governance (Rennie Center, 2017). In addition to these practices, the MEP also offers services and programs to foster relationships between school committees, districts, and teacher union leaders. Focus is given to improving student achievement and postsecondary success through training and facilitation in collective bargaining (Rennie Center, 2017).

The Interest-Based Bargaining Institute, one of the MEP training programs, focuses on helping local leaders identify shared goals and interests and effective strategies for ensuring attainment in those areas (Ventello, 2017). Leaders who used interest-based bargaining (IBB) reported that negotiations were more collaborative, and union leader-superintendent engagement was better positioned to support improvements in school performance (Kochan & Bluestone, 2015; Ventello, 2017).

The District Capacity Project (DCP) supports local school districts in developing the ability to construct and lead advanced reform strategies designed to improve teaching and learning. Comprised of labor, management, and community leaders and representatives, DCP teams work collaboratively to ascertain strategies to effectively implement improvements, while MEP facilitators aid in the codesign and implementation of initiatives to enhance student learning and success; improve teacher commitment; direct school and district improvement efforts; enhance problem-solving and decision-making processes; and develop skills, structures, and policies to sustain collaborative practice (Rennie Center, 2017).

Within its first two years, the MEP saw improvements in labor and district leaders' views of collective bargaining and labor-management relations as vehicles for improving student performance, and it researched evidence on how collaborative labor-management processes are used (Kochan &

Bluestone, 2015). The use of interest-based bargaining can be successful in improving collaboration in negotiations and ongoing union leader–superintendent relationships. Both the Interest-Based Bargaining Institute and the DCP demonstrate the potential of intensive training and facilitation for improving teacher-administrator relationships and enabling labor-management teams to attain enhanced outcomes for students (Kochan & Bluestone, 2015).

The MEP continues to expand its reach and impact by working in partnership to extend advances and improvements across the nation, in hopes that the core vision and belief in collaborative labor-management relations becomes a critical driver for improving student achievement and school performance (Kochan & Bluestone, 2015).

Interest-Based Bargaining

Interest-based bargaining (IBB) requires teachers and administrators to work collaboratively to achieve solutions that are acceptable and supported by all parties (Ventello, 2017). The first step in the bargaining process is to clearly identify, list, and define each party's interests, followed by the development of mutually acceptable options to meet those interests (Ventello, 2017; Lum, 2017). During the brainstorming phase, parties develop creative options without prematurely committing to any of them. The best solution to an issue is then developed by measuring the suggested options against the established criteria (Ventello, 2017).

While exploring each side's interests, reasons, and needs, educators of various types—teachers, administrators, and unions—may discover that they share many of the same goals, including improved schools and better-educated students, more effective educators, and a more fair system of evaluation (Lum, 2017). Understanding each other's interests and motivations can help anticipate the concerns of each side and foster smooth negotiations in which solutions are formed collaboratively (Lum, 2017).

ADVANCING STUDENT ACHIEVEMENT

Collaboration is a shared mind-set and an agreed-upon collection of processes that, over time, enables everyone connected to a school to effectively work together in educating children (Anrig, 2014). Although collaboration may promote a self-sustaining culture between any individual superintendent, principal, or teachers' union representative, disruptive personnel changes and political forces can halt progress built on collaboration (Anrig, 2014).

Labor-management collaboration is necessary for sustained improvement in school performance, as well as strong relations with a persistent, team-oriented focus that enables teachers to work more effectively with students (Anrig, 2014). Close ties with parents and community groups, as well as assessment results that identify areas where students and teachers need more support, must also be considered if sustained improvement is the goal (Anrig, 2014).

The most effective schools have developed an exceptionally high degree of relational trust among their administrators, teachers, parents, and community service providers, as well as an integrated support network for students (Anrig, 2015). These same schools were found to have a coherent instructional guidance system that coordinated curriculum and assessment within and across grades and included meaningful teacher involvement (Anrig, 2014).

At the school level, administrators and teachers indicated that they worked closely together to develop and select instructional materials, assessments, and learning strategies. Teachers also set aside time every week to work together to systematically improve instructional practices and monitor test data to identify where students and teachers need additional support (Anrig, 2015).

In a study by Rubinstein and McCarthy (2016), compelling evidence was presented that union-management partnerships have important implications for the quality of education and student achievement that are attributable to greater workforce collaboration. The study found that building teams and creating collaborative work systems broke down organizational silos and increased lateral communication, information, knowledge sharing, and innovative organizational responses (Rubenstein & McCarthy, 2016).

School quality is a result of the interaction and collaboration between teachers themselves, as well as between teachers and administrators. Considerable evidence indicates that quality improvement in schools is based on improving curriculum and instructional practice, on analyzing student performance, and on making adjustments to improve learning (Rubinstein and McCarthy, 2016). Student performance, even in the most impoverished schools, can be significantly improved by institutional union-management partnerships and increased school-level collaboration (Rubinstein & McCarthy, 2014).

For leadership to be characterized as effective, a strategic focus on improving teaching and learning and attempts toward improvement must be grounded in continued efforts to build trust across the school community (Anrig, 2014). Leadership must be focused on cultivating teachers, parents, and community members so that they become invested in sharing overall responsibility for the school's improvement, and a clear alliance among interested groups is key (Anrig, 2014).

Traditional positions of leadership, such as that of superintendent and principal, have now been expanded to include assistant principals, teacher leaders, union leaders, and school board members (Anrig, 2014). A high degree of engagement between these stakeholders should be maintained to develop and select effective instructional materials, assessments, and pedagogical approaches to improve student performance and success (Anrig, 2014). Time should be embedded into the workweek for teacher collaboration, observation, and mentorship as an additional, yet necessary means to improve outcomes (Anrig, 2014).

ACHIEVING WORLD-CLASS STANDARDS

In schools worldwide, highly collaborative practices, coupled with a strong reliance on teamwork to identify and respond to problems, is associated with unusually strong student outcomes (Anrig, 2015). By working together, teachers and administrators are more committed and can achieve academic excellence as knowledge of effective practices becomes more widespread and accessible (Anrig, 2015). Evidence of demonstrated student success in strong-performing schools throughout the world includes effective partnerships, reliance on teamwork, and close attention to testing data (Anrig, 2014).

Stewart (2012) identified key factors that have enabled countries around the world to develop strong school systems. Countries such as Singapore, for example, have a clear and persistent vision of the importance of education, as well as the link between education, economic development, and social cohesion (Stewart, 2012). Canada, whose school system is similar to that of the United States, demonstrates that educational partnerships with key stakeholders, such as unions and teachers, is critical to bringing about policy change and reform (Stewart, 2012).

A study done by Ravani (2014) found that excluding teachers from policy-making is dangerous, as they have vital experience and knowledge from the classroom that no one else has. This is true in Finland, where 95 percent of teachers are unionized; this may account for Finland consistently scoring at the top of international tests (Ravani, 2014). Finland has clearly stated that without unions, it would not be able to secure and protect the rights of its teachers or implement any type of policy reform (Ravani, 2014).

The United States is falling behind, not only in the quantity of its educators, but in the quality of its education (Stewart, 2012). Because the United States' public educational system is decentralized and has variable standards and expectations, it may be beneficial to implement team-based approaches to changing organizational culture within its schools and establishing a common curriculum (Anrig, 2014; Stewart, 2012). Following China's lead, the United

States is taking steps to become more focused on teacher support and providing time for teachers to meet on a regular basis to improve classroom skills and curriculum (Stewart, 2012).

Although there is a general awareness of the need to improve the U.S. educational system, public support is lacking. States, districts, administrators, and other key stakeholders need to work collaboratively to engage the public in understanding the knowledge and skills that students need to acquire in order to be successful both in the academic world and in the workforce (Stewart, 2012).

Partnerships comprised of stakeholders from all aspects of P-12 and higher education, outside businesses, and parents will be needed to meet benchmarks set by other successful schools around the world. Developing strategies for identifying, recruiting, and supporting high-quality educators and leaders will be needed to build instructional capacity and design strategies to provide equity in developing world-class educational goals (Stewart, 2012).

FINAL THOUGHTS

Collaboration must include a shared mind-set of mutual agreement that enables educational stakeholders to effectively work together in educating children. In order to be effective, public schools should aim to build strong collaborative relationships between union leaders, administrators, and teachers. One of the benefits of a strong union-management partnership is that they are problem-focused and designed to use collaboration to create and implement solutions.

Throughout the United States and across the continents, unions appear to be improving the quality of services and academic support that students receive. This is good news, as school and union partnerships are easily formed when the proper techniques are used. Including all stakeholders in conversations and decision-making forums has the potential to make a significant difference in student achievement.

Administrators, teachers, community partners, and unions must be consistently engaged in extensive communication with parents to coordinate support for students that is attributed to student success. A sense of shared responsibility for school improvement among all stakeholders, union members and its leadership included, should be promoted along with trust built on student-centered learning climates. Using this recipe, communication lines between all parties will be open and shared, and students will thrive within a community of concerned, educationally minded adults.

POINTS TO REMEMBER

- Collaborative partnerships should revolve around the local need and culture of each particular school district, with support from local unions. To maintain a system of collaborative school reform and long-term union-management partnerships, schools will need widespread support from state and federal policymakers.
- Labor-management collaboration; strong relationships; and a persistent, team-oriented focus will enable sustained improvement in school performance, along with teachers' ability to work more effectively with students. Close ties with all stakeholders can help identify where more support is needed for students and teachers.
- There is some debate on whether union-management partnerships increase or diminish student outcomes; however, most research points to a positive correlation between the two.
- Countries in which union-school alliances are strong have more engaged teachers and students whose achievements rank higher on testing than those without.
- One federal teachers' union and the Massachusetts teachers' union, along with several other stakeholders, formed MEP in order to improve relations and student outcomes. They have several programs that encourage collaboration.

Chapter 4

Effective Professional Development Opportunities

Professional development plays a vital role in improving teaching and learning, and provides a direct link to improved teacher performance and student achievement (Green & Allen, 2015). Meaningful professional development should focus on research-based, pedagogical strategies and how to support all students in meeting curriculum standards (Marrongelle, Sztajn, & Smith, 2013). Components such as collaboration, time for reflection, alignment with other professional development initiatives, and specific items as determined by individual needs should also be incorporated into training (Geeraerts, Tynjala, Heikkinen, Markkanen, Pennanen, & Gijbels, 2015).

Professional development opportunities come in various forms, including professional learning communities, self-study or action research opportunities, mentoring or coaching relationships, and a variety of partnerships (Green & Allen, 2015). Each type of professional development opportunity offers its own unique way of ensuring that effective teaching increases and student achievement outcomes improve.

FEDERAL AND STATE REGULATIONS

Both federal and state regulations, including the Individuals with Disabilities Education Improvement Act of 2004 (IDEIA) and the Every Student Succeeds Act of 2015 (ESSA), prescribe the necessary ingredients for successful student achievement, including the use of evidence-based practices and access to resources. These same regulations stress the importance of effective professional development for improving teacher performance and, ultimately, student outcomes (Green & Allen, 2015). Many educational policymakers, as well as educators themselves, understand the importance of worthwhile professional development to promote excellence in teaching, skill improvement, and student growth (DeMonte, 2013). Under these federal guidelines, school districts are held accountable for providing valuable professional development for their educators (Green & Allen, 2015).

WHAT THE RESEARCH SAYS

Research (DeMonte, 2013; Bowe & Gore, 2017) has shown that professional development plays a critical role in improving teaching and learning. Meaningful professional development should promote the consistent implementation of research-based instructional strategies and should support teachers in ensuring that all students meet curriculum standards (Marrongelle, Sztajn, & Smith, 2013). Professional development must incorporate exposure to research-based pedagogical strategies and resources in order to increase positive teaching approaches and student learning outcomes (Bowe & Gore, 2017).

Most new teachers feel that their preservice education was insufficient to fully prepare them to be effective once they stepped into the classroom (Cannon, Swoszowski, Gallagher, & Easterbrooks, 2012). Ongoing professional development opportunities reinforce the continual growth of new teachers, as well as experienced educators, and must allow for reflection time, individual needs, and a focus on school goals (Earley & Porritt, 2013; Lauer, Christopher, Firpo-Triplett, & Buchting, 2014). Engagement in collaborative activities, mentorship, and meaningful professional development opportunities are vital ways to support all teachers throughout their careers (Geeraerts, Tynjala, Heikkinen, Markkanen, Pennanen, & Gijbels, 2015).

DeMonte (2013) conducted a study examining the correlation between high-performing schools and school improvement strategies that focused on supporting the development of teacher efficiency through engagement in consistent professional development. The study confirmed that high-performing schools that tend to focus professional development efforts on supporting and increasing high-quality instructional practices within the classrooms are more effective at raising student achievement (DeMonte, 2013).

COMPONENTS OF PROFESSIONAL DEVELOPMENT

The term *professional development* refers to improving teaching and learning through strategies designed to support, change, and/or develop teaching practices (Green & Allen, 2015; Lauer et al., 2014). Profound professional development opportunities should focus on the specific population of students served within the school and be relevant to instruction strategies and increasing student performance (Earley & Porritt, 2013). Unfortunately, professional development that is focus-driven and meaningful continues to be thin, sporadic, and rare across school districts in the United States (Bowe & Gore, 2017; DeMonte, 2013).

CHARACTERISTICS OF HIGH-QUALITY PROFESSIONAL DEVELOPMENT

Professional development is the link between the goals of educational reforms and the implementation and success of the reforms within schools (DeMonte, 2013). The Every Student Succeeds Act of 2015 recognizes certain components of high-quality professional development as critical to the success of teaching and learning. Components such as focusing on research-based practices, aligned with curriculum standards and student learning goals, must be intensive and continuous, must support school improvement priorities and goals, must be sustainable within the classroom and school environment, and must support strong collaborative relationships (Green & Allen, 2015).

Nine stages of professional development encompass a continuous cycle of professional growth. Developed by Bubb (2014), the stages are divided into three components, including:

- Domain of preparation: This embodies four junctures, including identifying needs, obtaining a baseline picture, goal-setting, and creating a plan of how to achieve the goal(s).
- Domain of learning: This focuses on two stages: activity development and the occurrence of new learning.
- Domain of improvement: This encompasses three stages, including putting learning into practice, an impact on student learning, and improved teacher self-efficacy.

Professional development is significant, as it leads to improvements in teaching, through effective instruction, and in student learning (Krasnoff, 2015). Positive teaching and learning outcomes through promising professional development can be supported by including key components in the delivery. Components include: a focus on content and how students learn, active learning opportunities, collaborative participation, and a sufficient duration. The link between teaching writing through valuable professional development is explored below.

TYPES OF PROFESSIONAL DEVELOPMENT

Professional Learning Communities

Professional learning communities (PLCs) embrace the idea of learning through collaboration, collegial partnerships, shared values and visions, and a shared responsibility for student learning (Bowe & Gore, 2017). Offering an alternative way to conduct professional development, PLCs that include the implementation of quality instructional rounds present an opportunity for improvement (Bowe & Gore, 2017).

Instructional rounds were developed by Richard Elmore (City, Elmore, Fiarman, & Teitel, 2010). Elmore adapted his instructional rounds from the medical rounds conducted throughout residencies; they consist of three phases that link problems of practice with improvement efforts (Bowe & Gore, 2017). Such instructional rounds were "designed to bring discussions of instruction directly into the process of school improvement.... It creates a common discipline and focus among practitioners with a common purpose and set of problems" (City, Elmore, Fiarman, & Teitel, 2010, p. 3).

A close examination of the phases of instructional rounds reveals similarities to the workshop model of instruction that educators often use in their classrooms. The first phase of instructional rounds includes engagement in professional reading and discussion, in which educators are able to learn about teaching and learning (Bowe & Gore, 2017). The second phase involves classroom observations and is critical, as educators reflect on lessons and how they relate to their own classroom practices (Bowe & Gore, 2017). The third and final phase occurs when educators come back together to engage in conversation while analyzing the observed teaching as a means to improve their own (Bowe & Gore, 2017).

The use of professional learning communities with the implementation of instructional rounds may be useful for improving instruction in writing. In instructional rounds that were implemented as described above, for example, teachers would start by reading an article or chapter pertaining to writing instruction, such as on the topic of a specific writing strategy. After the reading and initial discussion, teachers would then perform the "rounds," and then reconvene to discuss what they observed in relation to the writing strategy and how this will improve their own practice. This continuous cycle provides a sound method of learning, observation, and reflection that allows for improved outcomes.

Self-Study

It is important for educators to actively engage in research that will improve teaching and learning in the classrooms (Vanassche & Kelchtermans, 2016). Mills (2018) defined action research as systemic by nature, helping the teacher researcher to gather information that will improve personal teaching practices and school systems. The information is collected as a way to gain insight, to develop a practice in which staff is reflective and where positive change in the environment and student outcomes is possible.

Action research is a form of self-study, as it involves an educator identifying an area of concern or focus related to teaching and learning. The educator collects and analyzes data related to the chosen focus, interprets the data, then develops a plan of action (Mills, 2018; Vanassche & Kelchtermans, 2016). Action research can be conducted individually or within a group of educators who may have similar concerns. Some of the benefits of conducting action research include meeting individual professional practice needs, identifying and addressing individual student learning needs, and engagement in continuous learning experiences through professional development opportunities (Annenberg Learner, n.d.).

Mentorship and Coaching

The importance of strong mentorship and/or coaching relationships to reverse high teacher turnover rates cannot be denied, as it provides guidance and support and it fosters positive experiences (Marshall et al., 2013). The contributing factors to teachers leaving the profession within the first few years include a lack of emotional support and inadequate resources and materials (Marshall et al., 2013).

Effective professional development should instruct teachers in evidence-based instructional practices proven to support student achievement (Ficarra & Quinn, 2014). Educators who are explicitly taught these instructional practices, through mentorship or through coaching partnerships that include modeling, ongoing support, and feedback, are more likely to produce positive student outcomes (Desimone & Pak, 2017).

Peer group mentoring, as developed in Finland, supports professional development efforts by strengthening teacher efficiency across teaching careers (Geeraerts, Tynjala, Heikkinen, Markkanen, Pennanen, & Gijbels, 2015). Comprised of both new and experienced teachers from various schools within a district, peer group models typically have between five and ten participants who are responsible for planning, organizing, and implementing their own agendas for professional development (Geeraerts et al., 2015).

Peer group mentoring and support systems have proven beneficial. Educators are exposed to various teaching strategies that offer different perspectives and tools, and they build trust through classroom observation, open discussions, and the sharing of ideas (Osten & Gidseg, n.d.). These can all then be added to the educators' personal teaching repertoires (Osten & Gidseg, n.d). Another benefit to peer mentoring is that it models collaboration and teamwork to students. When teachers are open with students about their desire to improve their own teaching through teamwork with their colleagues, they are modeling skills essential for success (Osten & Gidseg, n.d).

Partnerships

Collaborative partnerships between school districts and postsecondary institutions play an important role in developing, supporting, and maintaining effective professional development opportunities for educators. The benefits of these partnerships include those to preservice educators, but also to continuing coordinated support throughout their teaching careers (Colwell, MacIsaac, Tichenor, Heins, & Piechura, 2014; Marrongelle et al., 2013).

The National Council for the Accreditation of Teacher Education (NCATE) developed standards for professional development schools. The standards encompass essential characteristics by providing a framework based on a consensus of what a professional development school should include, and how to accommodate and develop such schools (Colwell et al., 2014). The NCATE standards include five focus areas: Standard 1: Learning Community; Standard 2: Accountability and Quality Assurance; Standard 3: Collaboration; Standard 4: Diversity and Equity; and Standard 5: Structure, Resources, and Roles (Colwell et al., 2014).

A qualitative study (Colwell et al., 2014) examined the perspective of the NCATE standards from school principals and their partnerships with local colleges and universities. Four critical themes emerged: the relevance of professional development activities; collaboration and partnership; planned and data-driven professional development activities; and professional development activities that are aligned with what is occurring in the classrooms.

The results of this study (Colwell et al., 2014) indicate that the NCATE standards do play an important role in ensuring the sustainability of professional development partnerships. Data collected from both school principals and their college partners indicated agreement in the importance in Standards 1, 2, and 3 to sustain effective partnerships. Similarly, although both groups felt Standards 4 and 5 were important, they played less of a role in guaranteeing the stability of the partnership (Colwell et al., 2014).

FINAL THOUGHTS

Federal regulations ensure the consistent engagement of educators in meaningful professional development. The success of professional development opportunities supports excellence in educator performance and increased student achievement outcomes (DeMonte, 2013; Green & Allen, 2015).

For professional development to be beneficial, it should be intense, focused, aligned, and continuous; it should not be given in a one-and-done fashion, which does not work to improve teacher practice or student growth. The best professional development should focus on providing exposure to research-based practices that are aligned with curriculum standards, as well as training that builds strong collegial relationships, which are shown to increase teacher effectiveness, student achievement, and teacher retention rates (Earley & Porritt, 2013; Green & Allen, 2015; Harris et al., 2012).

Traditional professional development sessions have failed to increase excellence in teaching or improve student achievement because they have been delivered in sporadic and inconsistent ways (Bowe & Gore, 2017; DeMonte, 2013). There are several promising approaches to nontraditional practices of professional development, such as professional learning communities, self-study and action research opportunities, mentoring relationships, and professional development partnerships.

Professional learning communities incorporate learning through the building of collegial relationships and shared visions (Bowe & Gore, 2017). The implementation of action research provides opportunities for individual professional growth, as well as meeting individual student and/or class needs (Mills, 2018; Vanassche & Kelchtermans, 2016).

Mentoring partnerships foster positive experiences through guidance and support. Mentoring relationships can consist of one-on-one or group models. Peer group mentoring offers several benefits, including the building of trust, the sharing of ideas, and the modeling of collaboration and teamwork as essential skills for success (Marshal et al., 2013; Osten & Gidseg, n.d.). Professional development partnerships link school districts with local colleges and universities in order to collaboratively develop, implement, and support professional development activities, all of which lead to positive outcomes for students (Colwell et al., 2014).

POINTS TO REMEMBER

- Professional development that is focused, targeted, meaningful, and continuous plays a vital role in improving the ability of educators and learning outcomes for students.
- There are a variety of professional development opportunities available. Depending on the desired results, administration and educators may choose to use a PLC, a mentorship, coaching, action research, or a partnership model.
- For professional development to be beneficial, it must incorporate collaborative efforts, time for reflection, alignment with other professional development efforts, and a focus on individual needs.
- Components of meaningful professional development include a focus on exposure to research-based practices, alignment with curriculum standards and student learning, support of school improvement efforts, and sustainability across the school learning environment.
- Several forms of professional development have been proven effective for teaching and learning. These include professional learning communities, self-studies or action research studies, mentoring or coaching relationships, and professional partnerships.

Chapter 5

Promoting Academic Rigor in the Classroom Using Evidence-Based Practices

The pressure to raise student achievement has increased in recent years in response to updated legislation and a renewed interest in the need for higher academic standards as a way to compete in the global marketplace. The learners of the twenty-first century encompass a wide range of ability levels, and it is this combination of expectations and abilities that supports the need for instructional practices that benefit all students (Samuels, 2016).

The Individuals with Disabilities Education Improvement Act of 2004 (IDEIA) and the Every Student Succeeds Act of 2015 (ESSA) both require that educators identify and implement evidence-based instructional practices within their classrooms in order to increase academic achievement for a diverse range of students. Educators who use these strategies work to close the achievement gap by optimizing student outcomes (Scheeler, Budin, & Markelz, 2016; What Works Clearinghouse, 2017).

The continuous use of evidence-based instructional practices is key to providing appropriate, high-quality instruction for all students regardless of ability level (Maheady, Rafferty, Patti, & Budin, 2016). Research overwhelmingly supports the benefits of practices that are successful at remediating deficits in academics, behavior, and social skills (Scheeler, Budin, & Markelz, 2016).

WHAT ARE EVIDENCE-BASED PRACTICES?

Evidence-based practices are instructional strategies that have been proven effective through extensive and methodologically sound research studies (Council for Exceptional Children, 2014; Graham, Harris, & Chambers, 2016; The Institute of Educational Sciences, 2015). Strategies such as differentiated instruction, peer tutoring/modeling, and specific content area strategies provide equal opportunities for typical and atypical students to succeed in the classroom.

Statistics indicate that not all educational practitioners have been trained on how to identify practices considered to be evidence-based (The Institute of Educational Sciences, 2015). This presents a critical area for improvement in teacher preparation programs as well as professional development opportunities. The literature suggests that there are several strategies that teacher preparation programs and school districts can develop to address this disconnect; thus, it is important to explicitly teach, model, and embed exposure to evidence-based strategies in coursework and field-based experiences (Scheeler et al., 2016).

Differentiated Instruction

Differentiated instruction is the most commonly implemented evidence-based teaching practice used in classrooms today, and it takes into account content, individual learning needs and styles, presentation strategies, and assessment techniques in order to provide students with appropriate instruction. Differentiated instruction provides the instructional means to maximize student strengths, accommodate for weaknesses, and provide immediate feedback (Ford, 2013; Ministry of Education & British Columbia School Superintendent's Association, 2011).

Scruggs, Mastropieri, and Marshak (2012) define "differentiated instruction" as supplying students with the instructional strategies and materials that meet their individual learning needs. Teachers must employ a proactive planning approach that takes into account learning styles, needs, and interests, while also providing multiple pathways for learning, and the use of various assessment strategies as instructional guides (Obiakor, Harris, Mutua, Rotatori, & Algozzine, 2012; Tomlinson, 2014).

Differentiated instruction must also include explicit teaching of concepts using multiple avenues of presentation, supporting students to develop critical thinking skills, and providing multiple opportunities for students to actively engage in the learning process (Obiakor, Harris, Mutua, Rotatori, & Algozzine, 2012; Tomlinson, 2014).

Peer-Mediated Instruction, Peer Modeling, and Peer Tutoring

Peer-mediated instruction, peer modeling, and peer tutoring are similar terms used to describe a means of utilizing students proactively within the classroom. Students serve as role models and/or peer instructors to other students. Peer-mediated instruction is an evidence-based instructional model that has been proven effective through much research (Ford, 2013). According to the literature, there are two forms of instruction that peers can provide: direct or indirect (Ford, 2013).

When peers participate in direct instruction opportunities, they essentially take on the role of the teacher and provide explicit direction to their peers. This is similar to the concept of tutoring. Indirect instruction occurs through the use of modeling by the peer: The peer demonstrates a particular skill or task for the other peer. It is important to understand that when using peer-mediated instruction, teachers take on the role of a facilitator rather than providing the primary source of instruction (Ford, 2013). When utilizing peer-mediated instruction, teachers must also ensure proper "training" of the model peer.

Reading Strategies

Reading comprehension difficulties are among the most significant problems experienced by children (Kang, McKenna, Arden, & Ciullo, 2015). The National Reading Panel (2000) identified the critical skills necessary for reading development: phonemic awareness, phonics, fluency, vocabulary development, and reading comprehension. It is well documented that children must have a firm reading foundation, including success in phonemic awareness, phonics, and vocabulary development, in order to achieve success in reading fluency and ultimately reading comprehension (National Reading Panel, 2000).

The 2000 National Reading Panel report further supported the need for balanced and comprehensive literacy programs. A balanced literacy program combines teaching that engages students in direct instruction. A focus on phonemic awareness, phonics instruction, guided oral reading, vocabulary development, and strategies for reading comprehension are stressed as the most important components to increase long-term understanding in students. Balanced literacy programs support students' engagement in self-discovery, in allowing them choices, and in cooperative learning opportunities (National Reading Panel, 2000).

Kim, Linan-Thompson, and Misquitta (2012)

This study identified five critical components for increasing reading comprehension. Components such as the type of instructional methods implemented, engagement in self-monitoring strategies, combining various reading components within an intervention, fidelity in intervention implementation, and instructional group sizing all play a role in the success of reading comprehension for students who struggle (Kim, Linan-Thompson, & Misquitta, 2012).

Kim et al. (2012) stresses the importance of direct instructional approaches with opportunities for students to engage in guided practices as well as independent exercises. Direct instruction teaches skills explicitly and "involves drill/repetition/practice" (Stanberry, 2016; n.p.). Specific components to direct instruction depend on the subject matter; however, adding in strategy instruction often is key to improving comprehension. Strategy instruction refers to giving the student a plan of attack for a specific purpose (Stanberry, 2016). Once students are able to use the skill for a specific task, they are often able to generalize the skill to other areas of instruction (Stanberry, 2016).

After direct instruction, students are usually asked to work independently and should be implementing self-monitoring skills, such as questioning techniques. Students must be taught explicitly to question while they read. When learning to read, students should be encouraged to go back over what they read and ask, "Does this make sense?" (Morin, n.d.). As students engage in reading for the purpose of comprehension, self-monitoring questions should include: "Why am I reading this?"; "What do I already know about this?"; and "Do I understand the ideas and words in this?" (Morin, n.d.).

Any intervention to improve student outcomes must be conducted with fidelity. *Fidelity* refers to the consistent and correct implementation of the intervention. *Merriam-Webster* (2017) adds that "accuracy in details" (n.p.) is most important. The RTI framework (National Center on Response to Intervention, n.d.) adds that fidelity is the quality of implementation for any intervention. For this reason, it is vital that educators be expertly trained and then execute the intervention exactly as intended (Kim et al., 2012).

Instructional group sizing is another critical aspect to consider when hoping to ensure intervention success. According to research, groups of 1:3 (one teacher for three students) or 1:1 (one teacher to one student) are considered to have the best outcomes for students (Kim et al., 2012; Vaughn et al., 2013). Small instructional group sizing allows for increased student-teacher interaction, consistent student progress efforts, individualized instruction, and improved student engagement (Kim et al., 2012).

Hall (2015)

Effective inference interventions were examined by Hall (2015). He found that group size played an important role in making effective progress, similar to Kim et al. (2012); however, additional elements were found to be critical to successful progress toward inferencing attainment: (1) activating a student's prior knowledge, (2) integrating prior knowledge into current reading, (3) identification of key words or clues, and (4) using the key words in answering inferencing questions (Hall, 2015).

Before introducing new concepts or books to students, it is important to activate prior knowledge. To do this, teachers should ask students what they know about the topic and allow discourse to occur as a whole group or in smaller groups. By doing this, a student's schema is activated and ready to apply new learning (Carnegie Mellon University, 2015). Often educators will make a chart or a list on the board or on chart paper. This prior knowledge is used to assist with the comprehension of new material (Carnegie Mellon University, 2015).

Once teachers understand what students already know, it is important that they "activate" their schema and use it to help them understand new material (TeacherVision, 2017). Making connections between what students already know and what they read provides a strong foundation from which they can build a new schema (TeacherVision, 2017). Good readers "think about what they are reading and consider how it fits with what they already know" (TeacherVision, 2017, n.p.).

Using keywords and context clues helps the reader make sense of an otherwise unfamiliar text. According to Glass (2017), there are seven strategies that readers can use to understand the passage at hand. Word parts is a skill used to break a bigger word into two smaller pieces using the prefix, suffix, or a combination of the two (Glass, 2017). Finding an explanation or the definition within the sentence is another strategy used for context clues. Offering a synonym helps a student understand the text, or perhaps the synonym can be found within the passage (Glass, 2017).

Other strategies that readers can use to understand what they read include using examples to explain what an unknown word means, as well as using antonyms or opposites to provide clarity (Glass, 2017). Comparing an unfamiliar word to another word, or using an analogy, can be helpful, as can an appositive. An appositive uses a definition after a difficult word or phrase as a way to explain the text (Glass, 2017). These seven context clue strategies are useful to readers who may not have the fluency, schema, or skills necessary to read confidently. Helping students to learn and use these strategies independently will vastly improve their confidence and reading ability.

Watson, Gable, Gear, and Hughes (2012)

A summary of successful evidence-based strategies for improving reading comprehension skills for students identified as having learning difficulties was developed by Watson, Gable, Gear, and Hughes in 2012. Many of the skills identified by this research team were similar to others listed

54   Chapter 5

above; however, the most effective evidence-based strategies were explicitly teaching vocabulary, text coherence, and text structure (Watson et al., 2012).

Explicitly teaching difficult vocabulary prior to reading is beneficial to students who struggle with reading. According to Glende (2013), students who struggle with reading should be given direct vocabulary instruction in which they see difficult words repeatedly in different contexts. The word should be used in context and then given meaning to reinforce understanding (Glende, 2013). Using text structure and coherence helps students understand the words; however, most important is that students become adept at utilizing strategies independently, thus taking ownership of their reading and comprehension (Glende, 2013).

Writing Strategies

Proficiency in writing and well-developed writing skills are necessary for students to be successful in college and career readiness (Flanagan & Bouck, 2015; Troia & Olinghouse, 2013). The Common Core State Standards place great emphasis on writing outcomes for all types of learners. These writing outcomes are a fairly new mandate in education. Disturbing evidence indicates that 74 percent of students in grades eight and twelve are below the proficiency level in writing (Harris & Graham, 2013; National Center for Education Statistics, 2012).

The writing process involves complex skills, including cognitive, linguistic, affective, and behavioral knowledge, which must work in harmony together (Harris & Graham, 2013; Troia & Olinghouse, 2013). Most students, especially those with learning disabilities or who have limited proficiency in English, struggle with writing. For far too many students, the writing process can be frustrating, unappealing, and sluggish.

Research shows that students who experience difficulty in developing reading proficiency will likely experience ongoing difficulty with writing (Harris & Graham, 2013; Troia & Olinghouse, 2013). Struggling students and those with disabilities may experience difficulties in written expression, spelling, grammar, organizing their thoughts, and handwriting (Connelly & Dockrell, 2016). Teachers can support gains through the use of evidence-based writing strategies such as self-regulation strategy development, incorporation of a writing workshop model, and explicit instruction in the various writing strategies (Harris, Graham, Aitken, Barkel, Houston, & Ray, 2017).

Math Strategies

Approximately 3 to 9 percent of school-aged children are identified as having difficulties in mathematics (Watson & Gable, 2013). Creating representations, completing mathematical operations, and applying math concepts are often problematic for students. According to the National Assessment of Educational Progress (2015), an alarming 80 percent of fourth grade and 92 percent of eighth grade students with disabilities are at or below basic levels of mathematics proficiency.

A well-researched strategy for supporting students who struggle with mathematics is known as the *concrete representational abstract* (CRA) framework (Agrawal & Morin, 2016; Strickland & Maccini, 2013). This framework assists teachers in guiding students through mathematical concepts using manipulatives, visuals, and abstract notation (Flores, Hinton, Strozier, & Terry, 2014).

Manipulatives within the CRA framework are physical representations that allow students to engage in hands-on learning activities. The visual representations can consist of pictures of manipulatives or the use of virtual manipulatives. Visual manipulatives engage students in the representational phase of learning math concepts (Agrawal & Morin, 2016; Satsangi & Bouck, 2014).

FINAL THOUGHTS

The Individuals with Disabilities Education Improvement Act of 2004 and the Every Student Succeeds Act (2015) both mandate the use of evidence-based practices to support student growth. Comprehensive research has supported the use of these strategies as a way to close the achievement gap by providing appropriate supports for a diverse population of students (Maheady et al., 2016; Samuels, 2016; Scheeler et al., 2016).

It is critical that teachers consistently utilize evidence-based strategies across all content areas in order to address the diverse learning needs, abilities, and interests within the classroom. Some examples of successful evidence-based practices include differentiated instruction, peer-mediated modeling and instruction, and content-specific strategies (Ford, 2013; Obiakor, 2012; Tomlinson, 2014).

Reading strategies focus on increases in vocabulary and comprehension while writing looks to increase written expression, grammar, and organization. The concrete representational abstract framework employs the use of manipulatives and visuals to enhance math concepts. Educators must become knowledgeable about numerous strategies in all content areas, as both typical and atypical students can benefit from learning new skills to increase understanding and academic outcomes.

POINTS TO REMEMBER

- The identification and implementation of high-quality evidence-based practices are mandated under federal regulations. High academic standards, combined with the pressure to raise student achievement, support the need for evidence-based practices as a requirement.
- Evidence-based practices are identified through extensive research and criteria established by standards. Evidence-based practices are extremely effective at producing positive results for specific populations of students.
- Through the consistent use of evidence-based strategies, the achievement gap can be closed by successfully remediating deficits in academics, behavior, and social skills.
- Evidence-based practices specific to certain content areas such as balanced literacy programs, self-monitoring strategies, and the concrete representational abstract strategy are beneficial for helping students with learning disabilities, as well as struggling students, within an RTI framework.
- A variety of reading strategies, including using schema, context clues, vocabulary instruction, self-monitoring, word chunking, and small group instruction, can be taught to struggling students.

Chapter 6

Innovative Instruction and Assessment Practices to Advance Student Outcomes

Many influences contribute to a student's academic performance, including, but not limited to, personal characteristics, family, socioeconomic status, socio-emotional well-being, and others that are outside the school's control. Employing highly qualified educators is of utmost importance, and many local, state, and federal policies are designed to promote teacher quality and level the playing field among students (Hamilton, 2017).

According to recent research (Hamilton, 2017), some teachers are more effective than their colleagues in teaching using high-leverage instructional methods, and that translates into higher standards of achievement for the students in their classrooms (Hamilton, 2017). Effective teachers are not readily identified based on their education or licensing status, or by how long they have been in education. The best indicator of whether a teacher is effective is to examine student performance in the classroom as evidenced by scores on achievement tests (Hamilton, 2017).

TEACHING MODELS

A variety of teaching models improve student outcomes. Based on district, school, or teacher preference, each model can be chosen to improve teaching practice, fulfill gaps in learning, or provide differentiated learning situations for students. Co-teaching, project-based learning, Universal Design for Learning, direct instruction, and interdisciplinary learning all provide unique opportunities for educators and students alike.

Co-teaching Models

Co-teaching is the practice of pairing teachers together in a classroom to share equal responsibility for the tasks of planning, instructing, and assessing students, and it is most often implemented in inclusion classrooms where general and special education teachers are paired together (Trites, 2017; Solis, Vaughn, Swanson, & McCulley, 2012).

Classrooms with co-teachers provide more opportunities for one-on-one interaction between teachers and students, which can lead to stronger relationships, more student motivation, and increased engagement in learning (Trites, 2017). All students in an inclusion classroom will benefit from the additional support and resources, while theoretically being exposed to stronger, more creative lessons (Trites, 2017).

Co-teaching partnerships can be formatted in a variety of ways. In the one-teach/one-observe model, one teacher instructs while the other observes students to identify issues and assess performance. This type of partnership allows the observing teacher the opportunity to provide feedback on the effectiveness of content and activities, which, in turn, allows both teachers the time to improve teaching methods to meet the needs of all students (Trites, 2017; Solis, Vaughn, Swanson, & McCulley, 2012). Similarly, in the one-teach/one-drift model, while one teacher is instructing the classroom, the other provides additional assistance and support as needed (Trites, 2017).

Several co-teaching methods involve dividing students into small groups. In the station teaching model, the lesson is divided into segments and each teacher instructs part of the lesson at separate stations or rotates between groups of students. This method enables the teachers to provide specialized support in the content areas in which they have expertise (Trites, 2017). In parallel teaching, each teacher instructs an individual group of students in exactly the same way and at the same time, so that there is closer supervision of each student and more opportunity for student-teacher interaction (Trites, 2017). Alternate teaching may also be used when a small group requires more specialized attention and additional support than the majority of students (Trites, 2017).

Co-teachers are not required to use the same model of teaching every day in the classroom. If teachers have a particularly strong relationship, they may choose to share responsibility and deliver instruction at the same time as a team. The method of co-teaching used is determined by each teacher's unique style of teaching, the unique needs of the classroom, and the material being taught (Trites, 2017; Solis, Vaughn, Swanson, & McCulley, 2012).

Project-based Learning

Project-based learning (PBL) is a method of learning in which students are directed to identify and research a real-world problem and develop a solution using supporting evidence (Young, Jean, & Quayson, 2018; Young & Jean, 2017). What makes PBL unique is sustained inquiry, reflection, and feedback that help to solidify the learning. Once complete, students present the solution utilizing a multi-content approach (Wolpert-Gawron, 2015; Bhagi, 2017; Young, Jean, & Quayson, 2018; Young & Jean, 2017).

By using real-world scenarios, challenges, and problems, students gain useful knowledge and skills, and they develop and enhance critical thinking, problem-solving, teamwork, and self-management skills. Focusing on the problem to be solved, students are able to make independent decisions, perform research, and review their own and other students' work (Young, Jean, & Quayson, 2018; Young & Jean, 2017). Through the use of collaboration, reflection, and individual decision-making, students are able to voice personal interests, concerns, or issues that are significant and central, not only to themselves but at times to their community (Educators of America, 2017; Bhagi, 2017).

Project-based learning is beneficial to students in that it allows control and can develop the opportunity for profound learning experiences that students can utilize in further education, in future careers, and as productive members of society (Educators of America, 2017). As an additional benefit, students are provided with the opportunity to develop skills in observation, research methods, presentation, communication, collaboration, team building, and leadership (Bhagi, 2017).

Teachers engage with students on a personal level when using project-based learning as the instructional method of choice. Uncovering students' individual interests and work capabilities, educators are able to help learners to produce high-quality, meaningful work (Educators of America, 2017). Teachers are able to assess student capabilities more authentically than they would using traditional methods of assessment, such as essays and exams that are solely based upon lecture, memorization, and recall (Bhagi, 2017; Young, Jean, & Quayson, 2018; Young & Jean, 2017).

Project-based learning has the promise to renew a student's passion for learning and a teacher's desire to facilitate learning in meaningful ways, and it is perceived as a significant means for connecting students with their school and communities. Through PBL, students are empowered, connected, and engaged in learning, and encouraged to make an individual difference (Educators of America, 2017; Young, Jean, & Quayson, 2018; Young & Jean, 2017).

Universal Design for Learning

Universal Design for Learning (UDL) is an evidence-based framework that combines research in the fields of neuroscience and education (Meyer, Rose, & Gordon, 2014). UDL is a proactive way of planning by integrating supports and choices into the curriculum and the classroom. The UDL framework consists of three principles: *multiple means of representation*, *multiple means of expression*, and *multiple means of engagement* (Meyer et al., 2014; Ministry of Education & British Columbia School Superintendent's Association, 2011).

Multiple means of representation allows for a variety of options for the way teachers introduce and present information. Multiple means of expression offers students choices in how they will show comprehension of what they have learned, while multiple means of engagement supports the development of interest and investment in the learning process (National Center on Universal Design for Learning, 2017; Kelly, 2014; Young, Jean, & Quayson, 2018).

By employing the principles of UDL, teachers can create goals that promote high expectations for all students, use flexible methods and materials, and accurately assess student progress (National Center on Universal Design for Learning, 2017; Young, Jean, & Quayson, 2018). UDL allows teachers flexibility in customizing student learning environments and curricula regardless of individual student ability and learning style, thus providing all students with equal access to learning, more inclusive classrooms, and multiple paths to success (National Center on Universal Design for Learning, 2017; Kelly, 2014).

Using UDL principles in general education classrooms reduces barriers and supports learning by encouraging the design of flexible, supportive curricula that are responsive to individual student variability. Universal Design for Learning also improves educational outcomes for all students by ensuring meaningful access within an inclusive learning environment (National Center on Universal Design for Learning, 2017; Young, Jean, & Quayson, 2018).

Administrators can also utilize the principles of UDL to strengthen learning engagement by providing multiple means of representation, action and expression, and engagement to teachers, as well as access to a variety of professional development opportunities to foster a deeper understanding of differentiated learning strategies for diverse students (National Center on Universal Design for Learning, 2017).

Teachers can promote this type of learning outside the classroom by serving on curriculum selection committees and encouraging school districts to purchase materials that incorporate UDL principles. Professional development is necessary, and allows for collaboration with other teachers on best practice standards around UDL. Educators are then able to demonstrate and share how they have incorporated this valuable tool into the classroom structure (National Center on Universal Design for Learning, 2017).

Direct Instruction

Direct instruction (also known as explicit instruction) is an instructional strategy in which a skill or specific content is taught precisely by the teacher (Archer & Hughes, 2011). This strategy requires that the teachers explain and model the skill, task, or concept being taught. After explicit modeling, teachers provide students with guided support and reinforcement throughout the learning process (Archer & Hughes, 2011; Ministry of Education & British Columbia School Superintendent's Association, 2011).

Explicit instruction requires several steps to ensure effectiveness. First, the learning objective needs to be stated clearly and in student-friendly language. This ensures that students know exactly what is expected and why. Second, the teacher explicitly explains the concept or skill that is being taught. Next, the teacher models the concept or skill. Once these components have been completed, students should be ready to actively engage in the learning process through guided practice. Guided practice entails the use of frequent check-ins, self-monitoring and evaluation, and student reflection.

Once guided practice is complete, students engage in independent practice (Archer & Hughes, 2011; Ministry of Education & British Columbia School Superintendent's Association, 2011). These steps show what they know, independent of teacher prompting or guidance, and when combined, ensure student learning outcomes and maintain positive results due to the focused teaching strategy used.

Interdisciplinary Teaching and Study

Interdisciplinary teaching is a set of methods used to teach a unit across different curricular disciplines. The most common method of implementing integrated, interdisciplinary instruction is the thematic unit, in which a common theme is studied in more than one content area (K12 Academics, 2017). Using the life cycle as an example, science instruction might look at changes in one particular species, while in reading, the book focuses on vocabulary and comprehension of those life cycle changes, and yet when writing, students are explaining what they know about the life cycle.

Establishing methods of interdisciplinary teaching has important outcomes for teachers. Schools have more positive work climates, parental contact is more frequent, and teachers report higher rates of job satisfaction (K12 Academics, 2017). Integrated instruction also assists teachers in more efficient use of instructional time and enables them to differentiate instruction based on individual student needs (K12 Academics, 2017).

Interdisciplinary study allows students to learn by making connections between ideas and concepts across different disciplinary boundaries. In this way, students are able to enhance learning by applying the knowledge gained in one subject to another different subject (K12 Academics, 2017; Appleby, 2015). This teaching style is maximized when educators who teach different subject areas work together to serve a common purpose and assist students in making the connections between the different subjects (Appleby, 2017).

Using an interdisciplinary approach to teaching and learning has several benefits, including highly motivated students who have a vested interest in the different subjects being woven together. As a result, student contributions are often rooted in life experiences, providing a valid purpose for learning. It connects the information to a real-world context so that learning becomes more meaningful and purposeful, resulting in experiences that remain with the student indefinitely (Appleby, 2017).

Students also begin to consolidate learning by synthesizing ideas from multiple perspectives and consider alternative ways of knowledge acquisition. Students are given the opportunity to work with multiple sources of information, thus ensuring a more inclusive approach to learning (K12 Academics, 2017; Appleby, 2017). Exploring topics across a wide range of subjects helps motivate students to pursue new knowledge in different subjects. Implementation of interdisciplinary study methods ensures students learn transferable skills, such as critical thinking, the ability to synthesize information, and various research methods, which are all transferable to future learning experiences (Appleby, 2017). When educators use an interdisciplinary method in teaching, students have a continued enthusiasm for the material being taught, resulting in increased attendance rates and improvement in standardized test scores (K12 Academics, 2017).

FACILITATING DISCUSSIONS AND USING FEEDBACK TO IMPROVE LEARNING

Research has shown that successful student outcomes are linked to highly effective classroom practices (Alber, 2015). To engage in these practices, teachers should clarify the purpose of a new study unit or project, along with the desired student goals and objectives, and the mechanisms by which students may be successful in achieving them. Providing visual models and examples of the end product will aid all learners in understanding what is expected of them (Alber, 2015).

Innovative Instruction and Assessment Practices 63

To be effective, teachers need to employ a variety of discussion and feedback methods. Facilitating a discussion will foster peer discourse and encourage students to learn from each other, as well as allow the teacher to assess student comprehension of concepts. Engaging in active observation provides an opportunity for the educator to offer feedback to students, whether it be individually or as an entire group during class time. Feedback is as important to students as it is to the teacher, as it provides an opportunity to understand how the instruction and materials may need to be adjusted for future learning (Alber, 2015).

Feedback from students should be more than the end-of-year evaluations that only summarize students' overall responses to the subject matter and the way in which it was taught. Student feedback should be solicited after each new unit or subject, and can be as simple as a half sheet of paper, or a quick online survey, in which students can list three items that worked well for them and three items that need to be improved or changed (von Hoene, 2017).

Teachers may wish to gather student feedback using short in-class reflection papers in which students can explain the most important things they learned and write down any remaining questions they may have about the particular topic (von Hoene, 2017). This classroom assessment strategy enables the teacher to see how students are processing and synthesizing the material, as well as what information needs to be reiterated or elaborated on before moving on to the next topic or subject (von Hoene, 2017).

Effective teaching involves seeking out numerous ways to reflect, and improve, teaching methods and subsequent learning (von Hoene, 2017). One method teachers may find useful in the critical self-reflection process is to keep a daily teaching log or journal of lesson plans and teaching methods, leaving room for comments and reflection in answer to such questions as, *What did and did not work well?* and *What will I change the next time I teach this topic?* (von Hoene, 2017).

Teachers must be encouraged to seek guidance from other teachers and administrators. Arrangements may be made for another educator to observe the class and methods of instruction, not as a means of critique, but as a way to gain perspective and share ideas on teaching goals, practices, and strategies for improvement (von Hoene, 2017).

Collaborative meetings should be held in which teachers can discuss ideas on the best ways to teach specific topics, and to exchange materials, resources, and suggestions on how to promote a more stimulating learning environment (von Hoene, 2017). Participating in professional development opportunities, such as online forums and workshops, and reading professional journals will also enable teachers to learn new ideas and stay up to date on current research (Kelly, 2017).

FOSTERING STUDENT SUCCESS

Although the definition of success means something different to each student, and it can range from simply passing a class to being an active participant in discussions and other activities, it should be a teacher's number one priority for the students. No matter how small or large the desired success is, there are several strategies that teachers can utilize to help students succeed (Kelly, 2017).

Teachers who cultivate an academic environment that holds all students to high but not unrealistic expectations will find more success. The establishment of classroom routines and rituals will assist students in staying on track and lessen the likelihood of misbehavior while allowing the teacher to focus on classroom instruction rather than classroom disruption (Kelly, 2017).

A rubric can assist students when given the opportunity to plan, organize, and monitor their own work, and direct their own learning (Alber, 2015). Encouraging self-reflection at each step, a rubric will keep students on task and allow them to understand the expectations for success at each level. Increased ownership of student work, and a subsequent connection to education, will occur if students are given the time and independence to become aware of their own knowledge and thinking (Alber, 2015).

Teaching methods should be varied to address student strengths and weaknesses as well as accommodate the different student learning styles found in the classroom (Young & Celli, 2014). Instead of spending the whole class lecturing to students, teachers should consider dividing the class time among lecture, small-group, and discussion-based activities (Young & Celli, 2014; Kelly, 2017).

Another way in which teachers can help students become engaged in developing effective learning strategies is to have students use self-explanation. In this method, students tell themselves what they are thinking and doing while actively participating in the learning process. It is best if teachers model this skill aloud, using self-dialogue and posing a question such as "How can I solve this problem?" and then work through the answer, describing each step they would take in its solution (Wilson & Conyers, 2017).

Enabling students to assess themselves through the creation and utilization of practice tests is essential to the reinforcement of learning (Wilson & Conyers, 2017). When students are provided the opportunity to demonstrate and teach what they have learned, they work harder, create and apply knowledge more effectively, and increase their capacity to remember information (Wilson & Conyers, 2017).

CULTIVATING STUDENT MOTIVATION AND ENGAGEMENT

Motivation and engagement are both critical in students' interest and enjoyment of school and academic achievement. When students are engaged and connected to education, they are behaviorally, emotionally, and cognitively involved in academics, demonstrate more effort, experience positive emotions, and are more attentive in class. High levels of engagement have been associated with positive student outcomes, such as higher grades and higher rates of retention (Stephens, 2015).

Teachers influence student engagement and motivation on a daily basis. Positive impacts, such as increased engagement and motivation, are felt by students when teachers demonstrate enjoyment and confidence in their teaching roles, pedagogical efficacy, and affective orientation in the classroom (Stephens, 2015). Teachers who display an elevated level of self-efficacy are more likely to engage in positive, proactive, and solution-focused methods of instruction (Stephens, 2015).

Teachers' enjoyment of, and confidence in, teaching has a positive impact on their affective orientation toward their students, as well. Positive student-teacher relationships result in heightened student motivation and engagement. Students who feel that teachers care and support student autonomy are likely to learn more, desire challenge, and be emotionally, cognitively, and behaviorally engaged in learning (Stephens, 2015).

There are several steps teachers can take to ensure that students remain motivated and engaged in learning. First and most important, teachers need to recognize and enhance their own mental and physical stability. To keep relationships with students positive, it is critical that teachers engage in self-care. When teachers feel good about and within themselves, they have more patience in the classroom and, thus, more positive interaction with students (Stephens, 2015).

Teachers must ensure that the learning environment is welcoming to students of every culture and students feel they are part of an environment where they are accepted (Young, Jean, & Mead, 2018; Young, Jean, & Mead, 2018a). Understanding students' cultures, backgrounds, likes, and dislikes will build rapport with students and provide teachers with ideas to foster motivation and engagement in the classroom (Stephens, 2015; Young, Jean, & Mead, 2018; Young, Jean, & Mead, 2018a).

Students should be allowed to work independently and toward goals they feel are important. When students have the ability to take control of their learning experiences, there is a marked increase in student confidence,

66   *Chapter 6*

commitment, and competence, which will subsequently lead to an increased level of motivation and engagement (Stephens, 2015).

To keep students engaged in learning, teachers should also create collaborative learning opportunities and experiences that are active, that are challenging, and that promote peer relationships and the development of social skills. Students are more likely to be connected and engaged in learning if they are reflecting, questioning, evaluating, and making connections between ideas and each other (Stephens, 2015).

MEETING COLLEGE READINESS STANDARDS

Research has uncovered evidence that the majority of teachers are not adequately prepared to make the critical instructional shifts necessary to meet college and career readiness standards (Marzano & Toth, 2014). It is essential that teachers and classrooms are able to make the shift in instruction that ensures students achieve the new level of rigor set through the state academic standards known as the Common Core State Standards (Marzano & Toth, 2014).

New PARCC and SBAC (Smarter Balance) assessments developed to test college and career readiness require more cognitively complex processing, and the subject matter and skills on the tests focus more on analysis and knowledge utilization rather than the recall of content (Marzano & Toth, 2014). More than 79 percent of teachers felt unprepared for the new testing standards, making professional development crucial to understanding the standards and developing innovative ways of teaching in order to effectively meet them and avoid dropping test scores (Marzano & Toth, 2014).

To help students succeed, teachers will need to make the shift from the traditional teacher-centered model of instruction that emphasized lecture, practice, and review, to a more student-centered method of instruction, in which students are equipped with the tools to work collaboratively in groups, or to individually apply and solve complex real-world problems (Marzano & Toth, 2014).

Developing the skills and ability to test hypotheses, to analyze and synthesize information, and to work collaboratively to utilize learned knowledge in real-world situations is necessary not only to be successful on the new assessments, but also to be successful in any future academic or career undertaking (Marzano & Toth, 2014). The Marzano Center's Essentials for Achieving Rigor model posits that, while many factors influence student learning, the greatest contributor to student achievement is classroom instruction.

Innovative Instruction and Assessment Practices

In its work, the Marzano Center (Marzano & Toth, 2014) has developed a number of essential classroom strategies for teachers to help students meet and achieve the rigor set forth by the new standards. These strategies include identifying critical content, helping students process content, helping students record and represent knowledge, and helping students practice skills, strategies, and processes (Marzano & Toth, 2014).

FINAL THOUGHTS

To promote student success, education will need to make a shift from the traditional teacher-centered model to a more student-centered model of instruction and learning. Academic environments and classrooms should aim for high academic expectations, and teaching methods should be varied across the board to address a multitude of student strengths, weaknesses, and learning styles. Teacher quality is essential to the success of students, and while research shows that some teachers are more effective than others, policies are shifting to promote instructional quality to level the playing field for students.

One way to enhance the quality of teaching is to use co-teachers and inclusion classrooms that provide all students with the least restrictive learning environment, that allow multiple opportunities for one-on-one student-teacher interaction, and that result in stronger relationships, increased motivation, and increased engagement in learning. Project-based learning opportunities are also integral to student success and long-term growth. The collaboration, reflection, and individual decision-making inherent in PBL allow students a voice on issues that are significant and central to their inner self.

Having control over learning provides students with a mechanism for profound learning experiences that will be carried on into further educational experiences, future careers, and the community as a whole. As a result of effective teaching methods and classroom practices, learning becomes more meaningful and purposeful, students become more engaged and invested, and success is achieved by all.

POINTS TO REMEMBER

- Student success should be a teacher's number one priority, and this is achieved through a wide variety of methods.
- Co-teaching, project-based learning, and interdisciplinary teaching are just a few ways to increase student engagement and ensure the student takes ownership of learning.

68   *Chapter 6*

- Students should have the opportunity to plan, organize, and monitor their own work, to direct their own learning, and to self-reflect. Increased ownership and a connection to education will occur if students become aware of their own knowledge and thinking.
- UDL enables teachers to create goals that promote high expectations, have flexibility in customizing student learning, and accurately assess student progress, thus providing all students equal access to learning and multiple paths to success.
- Motivation and engagement are critical to student achievement. Motivated and engaged students perform significantly higher academically and are more successful than students who are not motivated and engaged.

Chapter 7

Response to Intervention as a Pathway to Student Success

Response to Intervention, or simply RTI, is a federally mandated, multilevel system of supports used to assist struggling students who have been identified as being at-risk. The Individuals with Disabilities Education Improvement Act (2004) and the Every Student Succeeds Act (2015) both require the use of scientifically based practices, which are at the center of the RTI framework (Hoover & Sarris, 2014; Hurlbut & Tunks, 2016; Hoppey, 2013; Kuo, 2015). Support services, such as interventions and intensive instruction, can be implemented for a variety of reasons, including academic and behavioral (Mitchell, Deshler, & Lenz, 2012).

Response to intervention was originally developed to identify and prevent learning disabilities (Bjorn, Aro, Koponen, Fuchs, & Fuchs, 2016) and has since evolved into a pre-referral intervention pyramid. Through the use of universal screenings, students are identified as struggling or at-risk for academic failure. Students are provided with appropriate interventions, including ongoing progress monitoring to remediate any deficits (Hurlbut & Tunks, 2016; King Thorius, Maxcy, Macey, & Cox, 2014; Kuo, 2015; Sansosti et al., 2011).

Research has acknowledged the many benefits of RTI implementation, as well as its challenges. The benefits of RTI are bountiful, including lower special education referrals and earlier access to appropriate interventions for struggling students (Hurlbut & Tunks, 2016; Kuo, 2015). A lack of teacher training and support, inconsistency in RTI implementation across schools and districts, as well as limited resources are common challenges (Hoppey, 2013). RTI has been applauded for its ability to support the equitable distribution of educational resources and opportunities for all students, including diverse student populations (Hoover & Sarris, 2014; King Thorius et al., 2014).

70   *Chapter 7*

The RTI framework consists of three tiers of support. Each tier of RTI requires the consistent implementation of scientifically based or research-based practices (Hoover & Sarris, 2014; Hurlbut & Tunks, 2016; Hoppey, 2013; Kuo, 2015; Swanson, Solis, Ciullo, & McKenna, 2012). As students move from one tier to the next, the interventions and supports increase in intensity as well as frequency. The tiers are fluid, and students are able to move throughout the three tiers based upon their progress or lack thereof.

The interventions and supports focus on providing appropriate assistance for identified students. Interventions must increase student achievement in the identified academic and/or behavioral area of need (Mitchell, Deshler, & Lenz, 2012). The first tier of RTI works for approximately 80 percent of the student population and occurs in the general education classroom. Tier I interventions include the consistent use of evidence-based practices along with differentiated instruction (Bjorn, Aro, Koponen, Fuchs, & Fuchs, 2016; King Thorius, Maxcy, Macey, & Cox, 2014; Hoover & Sarris, 2014; King Thorius & Maxcy, 2015; Kuo, 2015).

Tier II of the RTI framework provides interventions for approximately 15 percent of students who have been identified as struggling or at-risk for failing through a universal screening. Tier II supports include specific and targeted instruction specific to remediating a precise skill area. Targeted instruction occurs through the use of evidence-based strategies, and in small-group settings within the general education classroom (King Thorius et al., 2014).

Tier III of the RTI framework is meant for approximately 5 percent of the student population. Students at this tier require interventions that are more intensive and targeted in nature. These interventions are conducted in small groups or in one-on-one situations outside of the general education classroom. Students who do not make sufficient progress at the third tier are then referred for an eligibility evaluation for special education services (Fuchs, Fuchs, & Compton, 2012).

UNDERSTANDING THE RTI FRAMEWORK

Throughout the implementation of RTI, general and special education teachers, as well as specialists, combine their expertise to ensure successful implementation of RTI. Within Tier I, general education teachers are required, under federal regulation, to implement high-quality, evidence-based instructional practices. General education teachers should engage in the frequent use of universal screenings, which provide ongoing data and identify students requiring additional interventions (Bjorn et al., 2016). Within some schools and districts, special education teachers and specialists, such as speech pathologists, may consult within Tier I, but their involvement should be limited at this level.

General education, special education teachers, and other specialists may engage in evidence-based interventions within the second tier of RTI (Bjorn et al., 2016; Leonard, 2012). Educators implement targeted instruction to small groups of identified students within the general education classroom. Occasionally, Tier II interventions can occur outside the general education class as long as notice is given to the student's parents or guardians.

The third tier of RTI requires special education teachers and/or specialists conducting the targeted and intensive interventions. These interventions occur outside the general education classroom and ensue more frequently than at Tier II (Leonard, 2012; Werts & Carpenter, 2013). Once a student is moved into Tier III, a referral for special education can be started; however, some schools and districts require the student to participate in Tier II for a period of time in order to collect data and monitor progress before starting the referral process.

For the successful implementation of RTI, student expectations, both academic and behavioral, must be clearly identified and stated. Furthermore, student learning assessment measures must be reliable and implemented consistently to measure progress (Sansosti et al., 2011). Academic expectations are easy to identify, as they are clearly stated in the learning standards. Assessment measures, on the other hand, can be inconsistent.

Throughout the RTI process, student data is consistently collected, analyzed, and used to make informed decisions. The team must look at the effectiveness of an intervention as well as whether a referral to determine eligibility for special education services is needed (King Thorius & Maxcy, 2015; Swanson et al., 2012).

RESPONSE TO INTERVENTION
AND SPECIAL EDUCATION

As RTI evolves, special education teachers may assume additional roles and responsibilities throughout the various tiers. Tasks such as increased consultation to general education teachers regarding all students, implementing interventions and progress monitoring for students not identified as having a disability, and frequent participation in RTI or pre-referral meetings may become a common occurrence for these specialists (Bjorn et al., 2016; King Thorius & Maxcy, 2015).

A 2012 study examining the viewpoints of special education teachers related to their roles within the RTI framework, as well as the strengths and weaknesses of the RTI framework, revealed mixed feelings (Swanson et al.,

2012). Special education teachers expressed positive feelings pertaining to the ability, through RTI, to identify the needs of students early and quickly implement appropriate interventions before students fell further behind (Swanson et al., 2012). Special education teachers felt that participation in the early identification process was rewarding (Swanson et al., 2012).

Special education teachers also expressed optimistic responses specific to the engagement in collaborative problem-solving and data analysis meetings with various colleagues (Swanson et al., 2012). The special education teachers in this study felt that this secured their role within the school community, yet they acknowledged that there was an increase in paperwork, larger caseloads, and a lack of additional support staff and resources (Swanson et al., 2012).

Another study investigating the opinions of highly qualified special educators and their instructional roles within the RTI framework was conducted by Hoover and Sarris in 2014. Their study identified six critical instructional roles played by special education teachers within the execution of an RTI framework. The six instructional roles include being a data-driven decision maker, an implementer of evidence-based practices, an implementer of social-emotional and behavioral supports, a differentiator of instruction, an implementer of instructional and assessment accommodations, and finally, a collaborator with all stakeholders (Hoover & Sarris, 2014).

Mitchell, Deshler, and Lenz (2012) conducted a study exploring the roles that special education teachers assume within an RTI framework. This study discovered four key roles: collaborator, interventionist, diagnostician, and manager. This study further revealed that special education teachers who engage in RTI implementation devote only 25 percent of their day to instruction (Mitchell, Deshler, & Lenz, 2012). This finding begs the question as to whether or not it is beneficial to have special education teachers heavily engaged in RTI. If only 25 percent of their day is spent on instruction, who is providing the other 75 percent of instruction to students with disabilities and who require services under an IEP (Mitchell, Deshler, & Lenz, 2012)?

Further disturbing statistics uncovered within the Mitchell et al. (2012) study indicate that, in addition to the 25 percent of instructional time mentioned above, special education teachers spend a third of their time devoted to RTI paperwork completion, a quarter of their time engaged in collaborative efforts, and approximately 15 percent of their time analyzing assessment and progress-monitoring data to determine eligibility requirements (Mitchell et al., 2012). The results of this study, along with others, offer critical data to support the decision as to whether or not special education teachers should be extensively engaged in the RTI process (Mitchell et al., 2012; Hoover & Sarris, 2014; Swanson et al., 2012).

Special education teachers have the ability to provide support and resources to struggling students as the instructional and assessment accommodator.

Response to Intervention as a Pathway to Student Success 73

Providing appropriate interventions for at-risk and struggling students levels an otherwise imbalanced academic playing field. Collaboration with all stakeholders, including general education teachers, administration, paraprofessionals, and families, is vital to meeting the needs of a diverse student population within RTI specifically, and in general education more broadly (Hoover & Sarris, 2014).

RESPONSE TO INTERVENTION, TEACHER PREPARATION, AND PROFESSIONAL DEVELOPMENT

The Council for Exceptional Children (2008), through its position statement on RTI, supports the belief that general education teachers should be the primary supporters through the first two tiers of RTI. Along with being the primary supporters, general education teachers should engage in consultation from special education teachers within the first two tiers of RTI.

The CEC further supports special education teachers as the primary providers of Tier III interventions (CEC, 2008). It is imperative, therefore, that teacher-preparation programs, as well as professional development opportunities, focus on appropriate implementation of evidence-based interventions, progress monitoring, and universal screenings (CEC, 2008).

FINAL THOUGHTS

The Response to Intervention (RTI) framework is a multitiered system that provides ongoing supports for students identified as struggling or at-risk (Hurlbut & Tunks, 2016). RTI incorporates universal screenings, implementation of evidence-based interventions, ongoing progress monitoring, and collaborative efforts (Hurlbut & Tunks, 2016; King Thorius, Maxcy, Macey, & Cox, 2014; Kuo, 2015; Sansosti et al., 2011). RTI was originally developed to provide a more streamlined way to identify students with learning disabilities, but it has progressed over the years to include the prevention of learning deficits and the support of at-risk students through remediation and early intervention.

The successful execution of RTI is not without challenges. The inconsistent implementation of RTI across districts and states can present variability in the services, resources, and students identified as needing services. In addition, there continues to be a lack of comprehensive understanding as to the components and flow of RTI.

It is critical that teacher preparation programs and professional development opportunities expose educators to the components and tiers of RTI. These can

74   *Chapter 7*

be taught through explicit instruction, embedded course assignments, and field-based experiences within teacher preparation programs and continued into professional development opportunities. This greater level of exposure increases the knowledge of educators and results in more successful RTI implementation (Hurlbut & Tunks, 2016; McHatton & Parker, 2013).

POINTS TO REMEMBER

- Response to intervention is a federally mandated and funded framework under both the Individuals with Disabilities Education Improvement Act and the Every Student Succeeds Act.
- Response to Intervention is a multitiered level of support for struggling and at-risk students. Students are identified through universal screenings as requiring additional supports and resources.
- Response to Intervention involves three tiers of supports that increase in intensity and frequency. Each tier of RTI incorporates the consistent use of evidence-based strategies, progress monitoring, and data-driven decision-making.
- A plethora of studies (Mitchell et al., 2012; Hoover & Sarris, 2014; Swanson et al., 2012) reveal that special education teachers believe RTI provides for enhanced collaboration with colleagues and opportunities to intervene early instead of waiting for students to fall further behind.
- General education teachers are responsible for identifying struggling and at-risk students through universal screenings and by implementing interventions at Tiers I and II, while Tier III often involves special education teachers.

Chapter 8

Early Childhood and Special Populations: Considerations That Impact Learning

Today's classrooms are comprised of a very diverse set of learners. Students with disabilities, those with limited English proficiency, young children, and those from diverse backgrounds present a wide range of needs, challenges, and dynamics. This makes it essential for educators to be well prepared, for inclusive environments to be successful, and for there to be positive relationships with all stakeholders in order to support the successful inclusion of all students.

Full-day kindergarten has been proven beneficial for all students, especially for those with additional academic, behavioral, and social needs (Cannon, Jacknowitz, & Painter, 2011; NEA, n.d.; Parker, Diffey, & Atchison, 2016; Rathbun, 2010; Young, Jean, & Mead, 2018a). Research has indicated that children who attend full-day kindergarten make more significant gains than those who attend half-day programs in reading and math achievement (Gibbs, 2013; Parker et al., 2016). This is critical, because additional research supports the claim that reading achievement during kindergarten predicts a child's reading progress later on in school (Rathbun, 2010).

Although there is a great deal of research surrounding the positive academic and social benefits of full-day kindergarten programs, it is alarming that only thirteen states require that districts offer full-day programs to families (Parker et al., 2016; Young, Jean, & Mead, 2018a). Inconsistencies exist in the definition, program components, and funding of full-day programs across the United States.

The Individuals with Disabilities Education Improvement Act of 2004 mandates that students with disabilities are taught in the least restrictive learning environment. It is of utmost importance that the identification and consistent use of evidence-based teaching practices are present in the general education setting to ensure the success of this population of students (Maheady, Rafferty, Patti, & Budin, 2016; Scheeler, Budin, & Markelz, 2016).

There are many evidence-based instructional practices that have proven beneficial to support the learning process of students with disabilities in inclusive settings, such as differentiated instruction, direct instruction techniques, co-teaching strategies, and Universal Design for Learning. Equally important, students with limited English proficiency bring a different set of challenges to the classroom.

With the increase in literacy demands across all content areas set forth by the Common Core State Standards, English language learners (ELLs) are put at a disadvantage for making effective progress (Johnson & Wells, 2017). Statistics indicate that approximately 65 percent of ELLs end up graduating from high school (ED Data Express, 2016).

Teachers need to have increased knowledge and support in order to provide effective instruction to this population of students. Within teacher preparation programs, teachers need increased exposure to culturally sensitive courses and diverse practicum experiences (Cho & Cicchelli, 2012). Within the school setting, meaningful professional development opportunities, including cultural sensitivity training and exposure to appropriate evidence-based strategies, are a must (Johnson & Wells, 2017).

FULL-DAY KINDERGARTEN

Research has supported the many benefits of full-day kindergarten. Positive outcomes, not only in a child's academic capabilities but in his or her social and emotional growth, as well, continue to be highlighted within ongoing research (Cannon, Jacknowitz, & Painter, 2011; NEA, n.d.; Parker, Diffey, & Atchison, 2016; Rathbun, 2010). Full-day kindergarten allows teachers to develop a better understanding of each individual child, including his or her strengths and weaknesses. The longer school day allows teachers more instructional time to devote to teaching critical foundational skills, which better prepare students for the demands of the Common Core State Standards (Gibbs, 2013).

Developing, supporting, and nurturing a child's academic, social, and emotional skills early can prevent occurrences of retention and lessen dropout rates later on in his or her educational career (NEA, n.d.). When teachers are able to thoroughly assess a child's needs and abilities, appropriate interventions and strategies can be implemented sooner rather than later (NEA, n.d.; Rathbun, 2010).

A child's achievement in reading during kindergarten is a strong predictor of his or her abilty later on. Extensive research has shown the correlation between successful reading achievement and academic success in other content areas (NEA, n.d.; Rathbun, 2010). If students are able to comprehend efficaciously, they will have an easier time understanding content-specific vocabulary within other subjects, therefore supporting success across the board (NEA, n.d.; Rathbun, 2010).

Full-Day Kindergarten Mandates and Funding

It is surprising that not all states require attendance in full-day kindergarten, despite the documented benefits (Parker, Diffey, & Atchison, 2016). As of 2015, only thirteen states required cities and towns to offer full-day kindergarten to families (Parker, Diffey, & Atchison, 2016). States that offer full-day kindergarten vary in their definition of what it should entail, and even the length of the school day. This inconsistency presents a disconnect in the development of foundational preparation afforded to children across the country. This is especially true for children who may be economically disadvantaged or who have a disability and require additional support.

In their study, Parker et al. (2016) identified vast discrepancies in the funding of full-day kindergarten. For example, states that require districts to offer full-day kindergarten may or may not provide additional state funding to those districts to do so. In addition to the possibility of receiving state funding, some states may require families to pay tuition to attend and some states may not. Furthermore, there are differences in the program offerings and quality. States that are required to offer full-day kindergarten have the choice to offer a half-day option, as well.

Benefits of Full-Day Kindergarten Programs

Components of successful full-day kindergarten programs include age-appropriate curricula, small classroom sizes, and a balance between teacher-directed instruction and child-directed exploration (NEA, n.d.; Parker et al., 2016; Rathbun, 2010). With the longer school day, teachers have more flexibility in deciding how to allocate resources and instructional time in order to provide the best opportunities for children to acquire the skills they need to be successful (Rathbun, 2010).

Rathbun (2010) conducted a study examining the effects of full-day kindergarten instructional environments and reading achievement. The findings indicated that certain classroom factors directly affect a child's reading achievement within a full-day kindergarten program. These factors include: the amount of instructional time focused on reading development compared to other instructional time, classroom sizes, student grouping techniques, and a balance of teacher-directed instruction and student-centered activities. A closer examination of each component is discussed below.

According to this research, Rathbun (2010) discovered that children in full-day kindergarten spend three-quarters of their day engaged in instructional time across all subjects. Further, it was confirmed that half of this instructional time was focused specifically on reading development. This supports the claim mentioned previously that children in full-day kindergarten make greater reading gains than those attending half-day kindergarten.

The findings in regard to class size were mixed, depending on the proportion of instructional strategies used within the classroom. For example, children made greater reading gains in classrooms with above-average student populations when larger chunks of time were spent in achievement grouping activities. On the flipside, classrooms with similar class sizes, who participated in more whole-class reading instruction, showed smaller gains in reading achievement (Rathbun, 2010).

Challenges of Full-Day Kindergarten Programs

The biggest challenge to implementing effective full-day kindergarten programs is the cost. With the limited funding options mentioned previously, making full-day kindergarten programs available, beneficial, and successful is a struggle. Costs associated with teacher salaries, teacher training and professional development, curriculum and assessment development, physical space, transportation, and school lunches contribute to the ongoing challenges faced by many districts (NEA, n.d.).

STUDENTS WITH DISABILITIES

The distinction of high academic standards in combination with the pressure to raise student outcomes, along with the wide range of ability levels within our inclusive classrooms, makes the implementation of evidence-based instructional practices a requirement (Samuels, 2016). Federal mandates, including the Individuals with Disabilities Education Improvement Act of 2004 and the Every Student Succeeds Act (2015), require that all teachers identify and incorporate evidence-based instructional practices within their classrooms in order to support increased academic achievement.

Another significant principle under IDEIA is that children with exceptionalities are entitled to receive special education services in the least restrictive environment (LRE), which in many cases is the general education classroom. Children with exceptionalities may bring a diverse set of needs, challenges, and dynamics into the general education classroom. This

Early Childhood and Special Populations　79

particular mandate also supports the indispensable need for educators to be fluent in evidence-based instructional strategies and models. Evidence-based strategies and models are available to support students with learning disabilities within inclusion classrooms across all content areas.

The continuous use of evidence-based instructional practices is key to providing appropriate, high-quality instruction for students with disabilities (Maheady, Rafferty, Patti, & Budin, 2016). Extensive research confirms the promise of evidence-based instructional practices work to close the achievement gap by optimizing student outcomes (Scheeler, Budin, & Markelz, 2016; What Works Clearinghouse, 2017).

ENGLISH LANGUAGE LEARNERS

The number of students identified as English Language Learners (ELL) is increasing at an alarming rate within public schools (ED Data Express, 2016). Approximately 65 percent of ELLs graduate from high school (ED Data Express, 2016). Teaching ELLs requires teachers, administrators, and staff to be culturally sensitive. Cultural sensitivity refers to one's knowledge and acceptance of other cultures and how they view the world (Johnson & Wells, 2017). When teachers are culturally sensitive, they tend to make more informed decisions as to how they can best instruct their students.

This increase has created problematic issues that need to be addressed through educational policy, states, and individual school districts. Two of the large problems include the achievement gap between ELLs and their peers, and underprepared teachers (Johnson & Wells, 2017).

English Language Learners and the Common Core State Standards

The increase in literacy rigor set forth by the Common Core State Standards presents a myriad of challenges for ELLs (Fenner, 2013; Johnson & Wells, 2017). With the focus on literacy across all content areas, ELLs are put at a distinct disadvantage to make effective progress without specific supports in place. For ELLs to gain a level playing field with their English-speaking peers, they require seven to ten years of direct English language instruction, as well as supports (Johnson & Wells, 2017).

Supporting Teachers of English Language Learners

There are diverse views as to the most efficient way to instruct ELLs. The first theory believes that teacher effectiveness is independent of student

80   *Chapter 8*

populations and that all teachers have a varied effect on all students (Johnson & Wells, 2017). Another belief supports the idea that teachers are most effective with students who are of the same ethnicity or gender (Johnson & Wells, 2017). Yet another theory suggests that if a teacher is effective with non-ELL students, then she or he should also be effective with ELLs (Johnson & Wells, 2017).

In order for teachers to feel prepared to instruct ELLs, they need to engage in culturally diverse practicums throughout their teacher preparation programs, as well as participate in cultural sensitivity courses (Cho & Cicchelli, 2012). Currently, teacher preparation programs, as well as some states, require multicultural courses on their degree audits, in addition to a Sheltered English Immersion endorsement (Education Commission of the States, 2014).

Once in the classroom, teachers need to be supported through meaningful professional development opportunities. To strengthen the effectiveness of teachers for ELLs, professional development should focus on two critical areas: instructional strategies for language acquisition and cultural sensitivity training (Fenner, 2013; Johnson & Wells, 2017; Zwiers, 2015). Content teachers, especially at the middle school and high school levels, need exposure to English language acquisition, as well as instructional strategies and modifications for scaffolding difficult content for ELLs.

Program Requirements to Support English Language Learners

Garcia and Morales (2016) conducted a study examining the components of high-performing charter schools. The authors combined their findings with the literature related to effective practices for ELLs to create a framework for quality programming for ELLs in charter schools. The study revealed inconsistent enrollment of ELLs in charter schools across the country; however, further research uncovered that ELLs who were enrolled in charter schools gained approximately forty-three additional days of instructional time in both reading and math compared to public schools (Garcia & Morales, 2016). This is due in part to the ability of charter schools to extend their days and school year.

As a result of their research, Garcia and Morales (2016) recommended a framework consisting of five components to promote quality programming and effective practices for dual language learners. The components include a coherent schoolwide model, focus on language development, building the capacity of all educators to teach ELLs, data-driven focus on continuous improvement, and family and community engagement (Garcia & Morales, 2016).

Early Childhood and Special Populations   81

A coherent schoolwide focus begins at the inception of the school model. School administrators must acknowledge and embed research-based strategies for addressing the needs of ELLs throughout the mission of the school at every level. Charter schools have more leeway in terms of design and accountability over public schools; thus, they are at an advantage for designing targeted programs specifically beneficial for serving ELLs. This allows for increased opportunities to attract, support, and retain diverse families (Garcia & Morales, 2016).

The second framework focuses on language development and is a critical step in the process. Educators must be familiar with, and engaged in, implementing research-based instructional strategies for building language development while students are learning grade-level content. The increased focus on literacy across all content areas within the Common Core State Standards places ELLs at a disadvantage; therefore, the focus on extensive language development and English language acquisition is a critical component of any efficient ELL program. One way to ensure this is through bilingual education, which is supported through extensive research (Garcia & Morales, 2016).

Building the capacity of all educators to teach ELLs is the third component in the framework. The number of diverse students in our classrooms is rapidly rising, suggesting the need for well-trained educators (Garcia & Morales, 2016). Teachers, through their training, must possess a strong knowledge of the content, be able to align curriculum with instructional practices, and use research-based practices (Garcia & Morales, 2016). Understanding the needs of ELLs requires educators to be cognizant of background knowledge and awareness, as well as the resources to support language acquisition (Garcia & Morales, 2016).

A data-driven focus on continuous improvement pertaining to the proposed framework means consistently collecting and analyzing data from assessments to create personalized learning plans. These plans address the weakness of individual students and specifically identify supports and interventions needed, similar to that of RTI (Gracia & Morales, 2016).

Family and community engagement is the fifth component of the framework. There are many ways in which a school can promote family and community engagement for ELLs. Practices such as communicating in multiple languages, volunteering opportunities, community partnerships, and heritage celebrations all connect ELL students and their families to the school in which they learn (Garcia & Morales, 2016).

How Principals Can Support Teachers of English Language Learners

For ELLs to experience success in school, it is important that school administrators are knowledgeable about effective instructional strategies and programming for ELLs (Padron & Waxman, 2016). This is accomplished through professional development opportunities for staff, providing critical resources to support classroom teachers, as well as hiring additional staff when necessary (Padron & Waxman, 2016).

In their 2016 study, Padron and Waxman examined the perceptions of school principals and their knowledge and understanding of the ELL programming in their respective schools. The study also examined the strengths and weaknesses of the ELL program models. From this study, two themes emerged: the key role that the teachers play in the ELL programs, and a lack of clarity and consistency between the programs in the study (Padron & Waxman, 2016).

The first theme acknowledged the importance of highly qualified teachers and, in this instance, highly qualified ELL teachers. Many of the principals in the study expressed the sentiment that the teachers in their program were of high caliber in bilingual education, committed to their students, and that teacher and parent partnerships were predominant (Padron & Waxman, 2016). Two negative findings under this theme pertained to limited professional development opportunities for bilingual teachers and insufficient principal knowledge to be able to support their teachers fully (Padron & Waxman, 2016).

The second theme looked at inconsistency and clarity between programs, and it is important to note the reasons why consistency matters. The schools involved in this study were located within the same school district and included twenty-two school principals. To develop programs that have a consistent structure, school leaders must begin with a clear mission statement that identifies the learning needs of bilingual students and how those learning needs will be met (Padron & Waxman, 2016). In totality, the two themes suggest that the quality of bilingual education staff and program consistency have a direct and substantial influence toward the academic success of ELL students.

FINAL THOUGHTS

Today's classrooms are a mix of student populations, including students with disabilities, those with limited English proficiency, and students from diverse backgrounds. As a result, educators need to be armed with the knowledge and

Early Childhood and Special Populations

support to provide appropriate and beneficial instruction to meet a wide range of needs and abilities.

Full-day kindergarten offers promising results for all students, including those who need additional supports and interventions (Young, Jean, & Mead, 2018a; NEA, n.d.; Parker, Diffey, & Atchison, 2016). When children's academic, emotional, behavioral, and social needs are met early and consistently, their success is inevitable (Young, Jean, & Mead, 2018a; NEA, n.d.; Parker, Diffey, & Atchison, 2016).

Positive academic and social benefits of full-day kindergarten programs, such as significantly increased reading and math achievement, are well documented in the literature; however, only 13 states require that districts offer full-day programs to families (Parker et al., 2016). Currently, inconsistencies in program components and lack of funding for full-day programs exist across all states (Parker et al., 2016).

Students with disabilities frequently receive services in the general education setting. This creates an urgency for the general education teacher to become fluent in the identification and consistent use of evidence-based teaching practices to ensure that appropriate learning occurs (Maheady, Rafferty, Patti, & Budin, 2016; Scheeler, Budin, & Markelz, 2016).

Students with limited English proficiency present a different set of challenges to the classroom. The adoption of the Common Core State Standards has placed an increase in literacy demands across all content areas, which presents challenges for English language learners (Johnson & Wells, 2017). Ensuring their success is vital to the classroom.

Teachers need to have increased knowledge and support in order to provide effective instruction to this population of students. Teacher preparation programs and professional development opportunities must require increased exposure to culturally sensitive courses, diverse field-based experiences, and exposure to appropriate evidence-based instructional strategies (Cho & Cicchelli, 2012; Johnson & Wells, 2017).

POINTS TO REMEMBER

- Today's inclusive classrooms are a mix of diverse student populations that present many challenges, dynamics, and needs. It is critical that educators are armed with the knowledge, support, and resources they need to ensure that the best possible learning strategies are implemented.
- Research has supported many academic, social, and emotional benefits of full-day kindergarten programs for all students. Benefits such as increased gains in reading and math achievement are highlighted consistently

84 Chapter 8

across the literature compared to students attending half-day kindergarten programs.

- Students with disabilities are receiving services within inclusive general education settings at increasing rates. As a result, teachers need to identify and implement appropriate evidence-based practices consistently, such as explicit instruction, peer-assisted learning opportunities, and collaborative teaching methods.
- English language learners present with a unique set of needs. ELLs are at a disadvantage for making effective progress in academic areas due to the literacy demands put forth by the Common Core State Standards. Teachers must be exposed to culturally sensitive training, follow evidence-based strategies specific to the needs of dual language learners, and partake in culturally diverse practicums within teacher preparation programs.
- A five-component framework designed by researchers to promote quality programming and effective teaching practices for dual language learners was found to be very successful at charter schools due, in part, to an extended day and year.

Chapter 9

The Importance of Social-Emotional Learning in Fostering Positive Outcomes

Access to social-emotional learning has been a hot topic in educational reform, as schools seek new ways to address the social and emotional needs of their students. Supporting the development of social and emotional well-being for students serves as a way of increasing prosocial skills and has been linked to positive academic outcomes (Espelage, Rose, & Polanin, 2016).

Approximately 20 percent of school-aged children are identified as having a mental health disorder (World Health Organization, 2017). At-risk children are at a much higher risk for developing a mental health problem. Children who are living in foster care, homeless or transient children, those living in poverty, and those from culturally diverse backgrounds are at a disadvantage for receiving services for mental health disorders (Young, Jean, & Mead, 2018a).

Individuals with mental health disorders often face difficulties with interpersonal and family relationships, struggle with participating in the workforce, are more susceptible to substance abuse, and are at risk for a higher rate of suicide attempts (Allen-Heath, Smith, & Young, 2017; Darling-Hammond, Wilhoit, & Pittenger, 2014).

A well-balanced social-emotional curriculum promotes five person-centered elements. These elements include self-awareness, self-management, social awareness, relationship skills, and responsible decision-making (Allen-Heath, Smith, & Young, 2017; Collaborative for Academic, Social and Emotional Learning, 2014). Efficient social-emotional programs also address bullying prevention. Bullying prevention curricula should focus on teaching prosocial attitudes such as empathy (Espelage et al., 2016).

There are many social-emotional curriculums, programs, and frameworks currently being utilized in schools. Programs and frameworks such as Second

86   *Chapter 9*

Step, Bibliotherapy, and the RULER framework have proven beneficial at addressing the social-emotional needs of students (Meiklejohn et al., 2012).

There continues to be a rise in the implementation of mindfulness practices such as yoga, meditation, and breathing techniques (Meiklejohn, Phillips, Freedman, Griffin, Biegel, Roach, & Saltzman, 2012). Mindfulness strategies have been shown to be effective at reducing the occurrence of behavioral problems and anxiety, and at promoting well-being for both students and teachers (Meiklejohn et al., 2012; Zenner, Hermleben-Kurz, & Walach, 2014).

The Prevalence of Mental Health Needs among School-Aged Children

According to the World Health Organization (2017) and the Centers for Disease Control and Prevention (2013), approximately 20 percent of school-aged children are identified as having a mental health disorder. Children with mental health issues are more likely (17.7 percent) to engage in suicide attempts (Centers for Disease Control, 2016). According to the National Center for Children in Poverty (2017), less than one-third of children diagnosed with a mental health disorder receive professional treatment, nor do their families.

Children who live in foster care, are homeless or transient, live in poverty, or come from culturally diverse backgrounds are at high risk for developing mental health issues (Centers for Disease Control, 2013; Padilla-Frausto, Grant, Aydin, & Anguilar-Gaxiola, 2014). Research has shown the long-term effects that mental health disorders, if untreated, can have throughout an individual's lifespan (Allen-Heath, Smith, & Young, 2017; Darling-Hammond, Wilhoit, & Pittenger, 2014). Difficulties with interpersonal and family relationships, struggles with participating in the workforce, substance abuse, and a higher rate of suicide attempts have all been reported (Allen-Heath, Smith, & Young, 2017; Darling-Hammond, Wilhoit, & Pittenger, 2014).

SOCIAL-EMOTIONAL LEARNING

Preparing students to be twenty-first-century learners through the development of cognitive, interpersonal, and social skills that are embedded in teaching is the focus of the most recent education movement (Pellegrino & Hilton, 2013). Social-emotional learning is significant in the realm of education reform and can increase prosocial skills development and positive academic outcomes (Allen-Heath et al., 2017; Espelage et al., 2016).

Social-emotional learning has been linked to increased academic performance and self-resiliency for all students, including those with disabilities (Durlak, Dymnicki, Taylor, Weissberg, & Schellinger, 2011; Nathanson et al., 2016). Understanding the impact emotional health has on academic performance will better prepare schools and teachers to identify supports to address the whole child and not simply the academic side (Gueldner & Feuerborn, 2016).

Schools, classrooms, and educators are facing new challenges within education. In addition to meeting academic needs, educators and schools must also address and support the emotional and mental well-being of their students (Malow, 2015; Allen-Heath et al., 2017; Darling-Hammond et al., 2014). Educators, administrators, and other school and community members must create learning environments that boost the social-emotional well-being of students (Allen-Heath et al., 2017; Darling-Hammond et al., 2014). Social-emotional learning is a well-researched means to accomplish this challenge (Allen-Heath et al., 2017).

Social-emotional learning provides a framework for schools to "systematically develop students' critical social and emotional competencies" (Nathanson, Rivers, Flynn, & Brackett, 2016, p. 305). Emotional intelligence is a combination of skills that assist individuals with identifying and reasoning with their emotions. Well-developed emotional intelligence helps individuals process their emotions in order to enhance their reasoning and decision-making abilities (Nathanson et al., 2016).

Educators are urged to incorporate social and emotional skills development in addition to academic skills development (Committee for Children, 2017). Social-emotional learning focuses on proactively teaching both interpersonal and intrapersonal skills development. Some of the interpersonal skills include engagement in positive peer-to-peer interactions and making and maintaining friendships (Allen-Heath et al., 2017). Intrapersonal skills include such things as identifying and acknowledging one's own feelings, actions, and decisions.

Five Person-Centered Components to Social-Emotional Learning

Social-emotional instruction promotes five person-centered interrelated components. These elements are essential to the cognitive, social, and emotional development of individuals (Collaborative for Academic, Social and Emotional Learning, 2014). Person-centered areas of social-emotional learning include self-awareness, self-management, social-awareness, relationship skills, and responsible decision-making (Allen-Heath et al., 2017). These skills are essential to the cognitive, social, and emotional development of our students (Allen-Heath et al., 2017; Collaborative for Academic,

Social and Emotional Learning, 2014; Durlak, Domitrovich, Weissberg, & Gullotta, 2015).

Developing self-awareness supports increasing students' confidence through a focused attentiveness to their own thoughts and emotions. When self-management skills are improved, students are better able to deal with stress, to control impulses, and to make well-informed decisions. The development of self-management skills incorporates goal setting and goal attainment and allows students to take responsibility for their actions (Allen-Heath et al., 2017; Collaborative for Academic, Social and Emotional Learning, 2014).

Social awareness encompasses the understanding and acceptance of other individuals' points of view and feelings, as well as the acknowledgment of social and ethical norms (Collaborative for Academic, Social and Emotional Learning, 2014). Relationship skills development supports the building of friendships and engagement in positive social interactions and includes the development of expressive language, participation in two-way communication and conflict resolution, collaboration techniques, and setting personal boundaries (Allen-Heath et al., 2017; Collaborative for Academic, Social and Emotional Learning, 2014).

Responsible decision-making incorporates taking responsibility, resisting peer pressure, and making well-informed choices (Collaborative for Academic, Social and Emotional Learning, 2014). Choices that are safe, ethical, and respectful of others are highlighted under this component of a social-emotional learning curriculum (Allen-Heath et al., 2017; Collaborative for Academic, Social and Emotional Learning, 2014).

Social-Emotional Skills Development through Bibliotherapy

The term *bibliotherapy* refers to a way of teaching through storytelling. The term was first used by Crother in 1916 and suggested that individuals be given certain reading materials that would help to expand their individual perceptions, and those of others (Allen-Heath et al., 2017). Stories, such as fables, have been used for centuries to provide a moral or some form of wisdom. Essentially, bibliotherapy is similar (Allen-Heath et al., 2017).

Bibliotherapy is grounded in the principles of cognitive behavioral therapy (Friedberg, Hoyman, Behar, Tabbarah, Pacholec, Keller, & Thordarson, 2014). Utilizing bibliotherapy assists with building the foundational skills required for social-emotional learning (Allen-Heath et al., 2017). Once foundational skills are acquired, students can make positive strides, developing much deeper social-emotional learning tasks.

There are two types of bibliotherapy: developmental and clinical. Developmental bibliotherapy includes using books and stories to address typically developing problems, such as conflict resolution, peer conflict, and friendship issues. Clinicial bibliotherapy, on the other hand, includes using books and stories to address more severe problems, such as abuse, trauma, suicidal thoughts, and significant mental illness (Allen-Heath et al., 2017).

Bibliotherapy offers teachers a convenient and practical way to address the social-emotional needs of their students (Davies, n.d.). Books relative to various social and emotional needs of children can be found within school and local libraries. Many libraries also have lists identifying certain books and their application to specific areas of need.

Engagement in bibliotherapy to address social-emotional learning incorporates several components (Davies, n.d.). The teacher must review, identify, and discuss any vocabulary or topics unfamiliar to the students. Once those become familiar, the teacher may include a pre-reading activity as a hook to capture the students' attention. Completing the story and lesson, students then engage in post-reading discussions and activities in order to practice and apply the skills that are taught (Davies, n.d.).

Developing Social-Emotional Skills through RULER

RULER is an evidence-based practice for developing social and emotional skills (Nathanson et al., 2016). The RULER encompasses a set of practices effective at providing a comprehensive social-emotional program that can be implemented within a school or across an entire district. This framework focuses on the necessary skills needed to enhance the emotional intelligence of students (Nathanson et al., 2016). RULER is an acronym that embodies five skills:

Recognizing the emotions in oneself and others,
Understanding the causes and consequences of emotions,
Labeling emotions with appropriate vocabulary,
Expressing emotions constructively across various contexts, and
Regulating emotions effectively (Nathanson et al., 2016).

Research has shown that the RULER approach is effective at enhancing student outcomes and improving the quality of learning environments (Nathanson et al., 2016).

Bullying Prevention

Part of social-emotional learning includes instruction in bullying prevention. It is estimated that 25 percent of elementary students, 34 percent of middle school students, and 26 percent of high school students with disabilities are victims of bullying (Blake, Lund, Zhou, Kwok, & Benz, 2012). The employment of a social-emotional curriculum for addressing instances of bullying by proactively teaching prosocial attitudes such as empathy has been established as beneficial to all students (Espelage et al., 2016).

There are many social-emotional curricula circulating around public schools throughout the country. One well-known curriculum is Second Step Student Success Through Prevention (Espelage et al., 2016). This particular curriculum has several iterations, each one specific to the age group it is meant to support: early learning, elementary, and middle school. The curriculum teaches prosocial attitudes and behaviors, school belonging, and academic achievement (Espelage et al., 2016).

Espelage et al. (2016) conducted a study with middle school students who have learning disabilities using the Second Step Student Success Through Prevention. The results of the study indicated that students with learning disabilities who were exposed to a social-emotional learning program, such as Second Step Student Success Through Prevention, displayed higher rates of prosocial behaviors, including intervening in instances of bullying, as well as increased academic performance (Espelage et al., 2016).

In addition to the Second Step Curricula, there is a Steps to Respect Cyber Bullying curriculum, available through the same company (Committee for Children, 2017a). This program focuses solely on the dangers of cyberbullying and how to implement prevention strategies. The program consists of five lessons, and includes lessons for the families, as well (Committee for Children, 2017a). With the occurrences of cyberbullying rising, this program would prove beneficial in any elementary, middle, or high school.

There are a wide range of social-emotional programs, curricula, and strategies out there to support schools in developing safe learning environments. Below is a list of several social-emotional programs worth exploring.

- *The Morningside Center for Teaching Social Responsibility* is an organization that supports schools in creating safe, collaborative, and respectful learning communities. They provide various resources, including lessons, videos, training, and articles, to name a few (morningsidecenter.org).
- *The Inner Resilience Program* offers K–8 programs for teaching mindfulness practices within the classroom. The program provides teachers with

the resources they need for effective implementation. The organization also offers support for families in the form of workshops (innerresilience.org).

- *Open Circle* is a K–5 evidence-based social-emotional program focused on helping students develop skills in relation to emotion identification and building positive peer relationships, empathy, and problem-solving skills. Teacher are supported through lesson plans and resources (open-circle. org).

Mindfulness, Meditation, and Yoga

There continues to be an increased interest in the implementation of mindfulness practices to promote wellness within our schools (Meiklejohn, Phillips, Freedman, Griffin, Biegel, Roach, & Saltzman, 2012). Mindfulness strategies include meditation, breathing techniques, and yoga. These routines have been shown to remediate problem behaviors and promote well-being for students with mental health problems, such as anxiety and depression, as well as occasional frustration or sadness (Meiklejohn et al., 2012).

A meta-analysis of twenty-four universal school-based mindfulness programs that focused on teaching relaxation and coping skills to all students, indicated that mindfulness interventions have positive outcomes on a student's ability to focus, regulate self-control, and ultimately make academic gains (Zenner et al., 2014).

Integra Mindfulness Martial Arts is an evidence-informed intervention that combines mindfulness, cognitive therapy, and behavior modification into a martial-arts training program (Milligan et al., 2015). A qualitative study of the effects of Integra Mindfulness Martial Arts to support self-regulation challenges for students with learning disabilities was conducted, and the results indicated that adolescents felt that learning and participating in the mindfulness practices provided strategies that they could use to decrease patterns of emotional dysfunction and self-regulate their behaviors (Milligan et al., 2015).

A 2008 study conducted by Beauchemin, Hutchins, and Patterson (2008) looked at the impact of a mindfulness and meditation intervention on the anxiety levels of high school students diagnosed with learning disabilities. The study consisted of ten minutes of meditation at the beginning of each class period, five days per week for five consecutive weeks. The results revealed significant decreases in anxiety symptoms and, therefore, minimized cognitive interference, which yielded positive academic outcomes across all participants (Beauchemin et al., 2008; Gueldner & Feuerborn, 2016).

Programs that teach mindfulness-based strategies can fall under the umbrella of social-emotional learning. Although mindfulness-based practices are unique in that they incorporate yoga, meditation, and breathing techniques, these practices offer similarities to components in social-emotional learning. Both occur within the school/classroom setting during a specific designated time, provide options for out-of-school/classroom practice, include the use of supportive materials such as videos and handouts, and can include parents and families in promoting practices at home (Gueldner & Feuerborn, 2016).

FINAL THOUGHTS

Social-emotional learning has been directly linked to increases in student academic performance. It is critical that students have access to high-quality social-emotional instruction. Supporting the development of students' social and emotional well-being increases their prosocial skills, which can increase positive academic outcomes (Allen-Heath et al., 2017; Espelage, Rose, & Polanin, 2016, Nathanson et al., 2016).

When schools are searching for a social-emotional curriculum to implement for students, there are certain components that must be addressed within the program. Teaching such elements as self-awareness, self-management skills, social awareness, relationship skills, and responsible decision-making are all effective at increasing prosocial attitudes and behaviors, a sense of belonging, and academic achievement (Allen-Heath et al., 2017; Collaborative for Academic, Social and Emotional Learning, 2014; Espelage et al., 2016; Nathanson et al., 2016).

In addition to the various social-emotional programs implemented in schools, there has been an increase in the occurrence of mindfulness practices. Mindfulness practices such as yoga, meditation, and breathing techniques have demonstrated effective results in reducing the occurrence of behavioral problems and anxiety, as well as promoting well-being for both students as well as teachers (Meiklejohn et al., 2012; Zenner, Hermleben-Kurz, & Walach, 2014).

POINTS TO REMEMBER

- Social-emotional learning has become a popular addition to most school curricula. Teachers are encouraged to support the development of emotional intelligence alongside academic requirements.
- Social-emotional learning has been linked to improved academic gains for all populations of students, including those with disabilities and identified as being at-risk.

The Importance of Social-Emotional Learning

- A beneficial social-emotional curriculum addresses five person-centered components, which interrelate with each other. These components include self-awareness, self-management, social-awareness, relationship skills development, and responsible decision-making.
- Evidence-based curricula, programs, and frameworks, such as Second Step, bibliotherapy, and the RULER framework, have been proven beneficial at supporting emotional intelligence.
- Mindfulness practices such as yoga, meditation, and breathing techniques have also been shown to benefit the emotional well-being of students as well as teachers.

Chapter 10

Engaging Families in Positive Educational Outcomes

Raising the next generation of students into successful adults and members of the community is a shared responsibility. When families, communities, and schools work together to achieve student success, the entire community benefits from these efforts (U.S. Department of Education, 2017). Strong family engagement is central to promoting children's healthy intellectual, physical, and social-emotional development, preparing children for school, and supporting academic achievement (U.S. Department of Health and Human Services and U.S. Department of Education Policy, 2016; Young & Jean, 2018; Young, Jean, & Mead, 2018).

Family engagement is the systematic inclusion of families in development, planning, and evaluation of school activities and programs that promote children's development, learning, and wellness and characterized by culturally relevant and sustained relationships between family and school staff in the shared responsibility of a student's well-being (U.S. Department of Health and Human Services and U.S. Department of Education Policy, 2016).

More than parent attendance at, and participation in, school activities, family engagement is the purposeful and conscious effort of a parent to engage in a student's education and development by promoting and assisting in the development of positive behaviors and ensuring a student's overall well-being (Young & Jean, 2018; Young, Jean, & Mead, 2018). This is not done in isolation, but with the support and help of the school (Young & Jean, 2018; Young, Jean, & Mead, 2018).

Family engagement is different from parental involvement, which is demonstrated by parents being told what to do; instead, the term *family engagement* implies that the responsibility for a student rests on more than just the parents, and can include siblings, relatives, friends, and the school. Although it seems that education takes up most of a student's day, it is only

96   *Chapter 10*

six to seven hours, and therefore, making family and community involvement and support part of a student's education is critical to success (Ohio Department of Education, 2016).

Parents and family members play a critical role in a student's education. Unfortunately, parents, especially those living in poverty, may need additional support structures to thrive as co-educators (Young, Jean, & Mead, 2018). One approach that combines a cohesive set of family, education, employment, workforce training, and related social service supports for parents and students is a two-generation approach. The goal of a two-generation approach is to lift families out of poverty and support the student's long-term outcomes (U.S. Department of Health and Human Services and U.S. Department of Education Policy, 2016).

The implementation of two-generation strategies may help to remove intergenerational poverty by targeting early childhood education and providing economic and educational services to parents; however, they do not always engage families as direct support in student education and rely more on preschools and other organizations for any necessary support (Young, Jean, & Mead, 2018). Federal and state policies may not sufficiently support two-generation strategies. While whole child-centered programs may focus on improving child outcomes, those same programs may not support parental economic success (Schmit, Matthews, & Golden, 2014).

Every Student Succeeds Act

The Elementary and Secondary Education Act of 1965 (ESEA), as amended by the Every Student Succeeds Act of 2015 (ESSA), requires that states and school districts involve parents in fostering positive outcomes for all students (U.S. Department of Education, 2016). School districts that receive Title I funds are mandated to write parent and family engagement policies containing expectations and objectives for employing meaningful family involvement strategies.

Family members must be involved in jointly developing district plans and providing assistance to schools on planning and implementing effective family involvement activities to improve student success (U.S. Department of Education, 2016; U.S. Department of Health and Human Services and U.S. Department of Education Policy, 2016).

Creating a Culture That Values Family Engagement

To integrate family engagement in school system programs, districts should foster a culture in which families are engaged as essential partners when establishing and providing services that promote student learning and

Engaging Families in Positive Educational Outcomes 97

development, nurture positive relationships between families and staff, and support families (U.S. Department of Health and Human Services and U.S. Department of Education Policy, 2016; Young, Jean, & Mead, 2018; Young & Jean, 2018). Family engagement practices can be anywhere from participation to partnership and have significant implications when activities are linked to student learning, particularly when there is capacity building and support for both families and teachers (Community Schools Network, 2017; Young, Jean, & Mead, 2018; Young & Jean, 2018).

To build systems of practice that establish meaningful partnerships between teachers and families, school districts should work with each school to adopt a strength-based vision. This vision should acknowledge that individual families have power and positivity to offer students and respect that a student's family is the first and most important, influential teacher, advocate, and nurturer he or she will ever have (Community Schools Network, 2017; U.S. Department of Health and Human Services and U.S. Department of Education Policy, 2016; Young & Jean, 2018).

Respectful and trusting relationships between families and professionals should be highly valued and promote a shared responsibility for the student's healthy development, learning, and wellness by placing value on family experiences and strengths. Opportunities should be provided for shared learning, and two-way communication welcoming information on all aspects of a student's life, including culture and traditions, should be encouraged (Young, Jean, & Mead, 2018; U.S. Department of Health and Human Services and U.S. Department of Education Policy, 2016; Lavoie, 2017).

Teams comprised of school administrators, teachers, parents, and other appropriate staff members are responsible for the planning, design, and quality assessment that occurs with coordination of service and activities. Teams use their common interest in student success to examine student data, create activities and goals, measure student outcomes, and assess the impact of its programs based on movement toward those goals (Community Schools Network, 2017).

Capacity Building

Capacity building for teachers must be a priority in education. By developing and utilizing a strengths-based approach, teachers will be equipped with the knowledge, skills, and tools needed to vigorously and successfully engage families in student education and success. Family engagement must be a priority in the overarching plan for teacher professional development, and school districts should commit vital resources to the effort, including investments in training, coaching, and mentoring (Grant & Ray, 2015; Community Schools Network, 2017).

98   *Chapter 10*

Professional development opportunities should train educators to view parents as capable, competent partners and strengthen their ability to form constructive, goal-oriented relationships with all families (U.S. Department of Health and Human Services and U.S. Department of Education Policy, 2016). Using a strength-based approach and skills developed through professional development, educators will have the capability of instilling best-practice standards within classrooms that will facilitate parent involvement.

Create a Welcoming School Climate

To create a welcoming environment and foster the connection between school and family, teachers should provide a personal greeting and welcome packet for all visiting parents that includes a community services directory, important school contact information, and school calendar. Teachers may also make contact with parents through e-mails, phone calls, or home visits (Young, Jean, & Mead, 2018; Ohio Department of Education, 2016).

Workshops and materials for parents on typical development and appropriate parent and school expectations can be developed, along with suggestions on what parents can do at home to support student learning and success at varying age and grade levels (Ohio Department of Education, 2016). Schools may also partner with community-based organizations to provide workshops on nutrition, family recreation, and/or communication (Ohio Department of Education, 2016).

During open houses, teachers should make themselves available to spend time meeting students' families and leave families enough time to tour the school and meet other families. Schools should also make translators available to welcome and assist families at the open house as well as at other school activities (Young, Jean, & Mead, 2018; Ohio Department of Education, 2016).

Establish Effective School-to-Home and Home-to-School Communication

Successful, responsive, and productive schools solicit, encourage, facilitate, and promote parental communication. In these schools, parents are consistently invited, consulted, and encouraged to communicate (Young, Jean, & Mead, 2018; Young & Jean, 2018; Lavoie, 2017). As consumers of educational services, parents expect effective, consistent, and proactive teacher/parent communication regarding student progress and performance. Parents expect that their input and opinions will be heard, listened to, and responded to in a productive manner (Lavoie, 2017).

School districts should facilitate two-way communication about student development, including cognitive, social-emotional, physical development, health, and wellness. Families should have the ability to share their expertise

Engaging Families in Positive Educational Outcomes 99

about a student in conversations and draw on experiences to suggest how they can help support student progress at home and in school (U.S. Department of Health and Human Services and U.S. Department of Education Policy, 2016).

To facilitate effective communication, schools should seek to provide printed information for parents on homework policies and best ways to monitor and support homework. Newsletters and folders containing student work can be sent home on a daily or weekly basis for parents to review, thus monitoring and supporting student work at home (Young, Jean, & Mead, 2018; Young & Jean, 2018). For those schools wishing to incorporate technology, electronic grade books can be developed for parents to monitor student progress at convenient times or in conjunction with the student (Young, Jean, & Mead, 2018; Young & Jean, 2018; Ohio Department of Education, 2016; Lavoie, 2017).

Communication about school policies and other essential information should be clearly communicated to families in their selected first language (Ohio Department of Education, 2016; Young, Jean, & Mead, 2018). Procedures on how to communicate with school administrators, teachers, and nurses, including direct phone numbers and e-mail addresses, should be sent to families at the beginning of the school year and again at the midpoint of the year. In addition, schools should provide multiple avenues for families to leave anonymous suggestions or comments, as well as a designated way for families to ask direct questions, share their concerns, and make recommendations (Ohio Department of Education, 2016).

Reliable forms of communication should be established, such as a parent telephone tree, or a designated parent representative, to provide school information, encourage interaction among parents, and keep families linked to the school and to each other (Ohio Department of Education, 2016). Research by psychologists indicates that effective, responsive, well-planned home/school communication results in fewer special education referrals, higher staff morale, and increased donations of goods, materials, and services to the school (Lavoie, 2017).

Strengthen Knowledge and Skills to Support Student Learning at Home and in the Community

Training should be provided for parents on ways they may help students improve study skills and learning. Regular homework assignments should be given that promote student and family discussion about what is being learned in school. Families can also be engaged in opportunities to discuss goals within various academic areas, colleges, and careers with students (Ohio Department of Education, 2016).

100   *Chapter 10*

Schools can also provide a directory of community resources and activities linked to student learning, including before-school, after-school, and summer programs for students. Workshops may also be developed to inform families of the high expectations and standards children are expected to meet, as well as ways for families to support these expectations and continue learning at home (Ohio Department of Education, 2016).

Engage Families in School Planning, Leadership, and Meaningful Volunteer Opportunities

Roles can be created for parents on all advisory committees and school boards, and equal representation should be given for parents on school governing bodies (Ohio Department of Education, 2016). Teachers can send home surveys to identify and establish parental volunteer interests, talents, and availability to match these potential resources to school programs and staff support needs. To recognize parent volunteers, schools can create events, certificates, and thank-you cards (Ohio Department of Education, 2016).

Opportunities for families to build knowledge around student development, learning, and wellness; to advocate for their student; to share experience and expertise; and to engage in leadership and advocacy roles can be built and provided through parent-to-parent programs, parent-teacher associations, and parent advisory councils (U.S. Department of Health and Human Services and U.S. Department of Education Policy, 2016).

Connect Students and Families to Community Resources to Strengthen and Support Students' Learning and Well-being

Capacity-building, an essential element of family engagement, is the development of relationships among schools, community organizations, businesses, and higher education institutions to collaborate, develop, and implement family engagement programming (Grant & Ray, 2015; Young, Jean, & Mead, 2018).

When developed, these partnerships will facilitate access to community-based programs to ensure that families have a set of appropriate resources involved in student success and learning. These partnerships can provide student mentoring and internship opportunities, as well as a connection to community services such as health screenings, parent education, and job training (Ohio Department of Education, 2016; Young, Jean, & Mead, 2018).

Schools should be actively engaged with community resources around children's health and development, their mental health, and their social and emotional well-being. Schools should ensure that families know about child development and have access to concrete strategies to promote child

Engaging Families in Positive Educational Outcomes 101

well-being at home and in the classroom (U.S. Department of Health and Human Services and U.S. Department of Education Policy, 2016).

Formal relationships, together with local community partners such as after-school programs, social service agencies, adult education programs, and libraries, will also help support families, promote family wellness, and foster student success (U.S. Department of Health and Human Services and U.S. Department of Education Policy, 2016).

Twenty-First-Century Community Learning Centers

This federal program enables the development of community learning centers that can provide academic improvement opportunities during non-school hours for students, particularly those who attend high-poverty or low-performing schools (U.S. Department of Education, 2017).

The funding requirements of the federal 21st-Century Community Learning Centers initiative enable public schools to successfully partner with community-based organizations to create programs connecting students to their homes, schools, and communities (Heckman & Sanger, 2013). Through these programs, students are assisted in meeting state and local standards for core academic subjects and offered various enrichment activities, while student families have the opportunity to participate in literacy and other educational services (U.S. Department of Education, 2017; Afterschool Alliance, 2017).

A comprehensive group of supplementary services intended to support and strengthen academic programs, such as drug and violence prevention programs, career and technical programs, counseling programs, STEM programs, and character education programs, are available to students and families (Afterschool Alliance, 2017). Programs funded through the 21st-Century Community Learning Centers initiative are vital to student success, as they reduce the gap between high- and low-income students in math, improve school attendance, promote class participation, inspire learning, improve homework completion and behavioral outcomes, and assist parents in retaining gainful employment (Afterschool Alliance, 2017).

Benefits of Family Engagement

It is well known that family engagement in a student's learning and development promotes not only his or her ability to learn, but also a healthy development, lifelong health, and successful academic outcomes (U.S. Department of Health and Human Services and U.S. Department of Education Policy, 2016; Young, Jean, & Mead, 2018; Young & Jean, 2018).

Research demonstrates that family involvement and engagement in a student's education is one of the single most important predictors of student academic success, and that when families are involved, students do better in school regardless of a family's race, education level, or income (Community Schools Network, 2017; Bienia, 2016; Young & Jean, 2018; Young, Jean, & Mead, 2018). Students with involved and engaged families are more likely to be ready for school, be more motivated, pay more attention, earn higher grades, attend school regularly, and pass their classes and graduate (Bienia, 2016; Community Schools Network, 2017; U.S. Department of Health and Human Services and U.S. Department of Education Policy, 2016).

When families and schools work together and support each other, students are also more likely to have fewer behavioral problems, increase their impulse control, demonstrate social-emotional growth, display a more positive attitude toward school, improve social-emotional adjustment, and show an increase in overall academic success (Bienia, 2016; Young, Jean, & Mead, 2018; Community Schools Network, 2017; U.S. Department of Health and Human Services and U.S. Department of Education Policy, 2016).

FINAL THOUGHTS

Creating, developing, and fostering an environment in which today's current generation of students will turn into successful adults and productive members of the community is a shared responsibility. If families, communities, and schools work together to achieve student success, not only will the student benefit from these efforts, but the entire community will benefit. Communities will also benefit if partnerships between families, schools, and local resources combine a cohesive set of family education, employment, workforce training, and related social service supports for parents and students.

To succeed in making families more engaged in student education, school districts and educators will need to share a strong, common vision and outright acknowledge and respect that individual student families, through their power and positivity, are the first and most important, influential teacher, advocate, and nurturer that students will ever have. Educators will thus need to make family engagement a priority and seek ways to improve upon family engagement strategies through professional development opportunities and the acquisition and commitment of vital resources, including investments in educator training, coaching, and mentoring.

Family engagement in student learning and development not only promotes academic learning and success, but it enables the student and family to develop lifelong partnerships that promote health and community engagement, thus enabling them to remain productive and active members of their community.

POINTS TO REMEMBER

- Strong family engagement in a student's education is essential in establishing a student's intellectual and physical health and social-emotional development and is shown to improve overall student success.
- Family engagement in a student's education is one of the single most important predictors of student academic success: When families are actively engaged, students will do better in school regardless of race, parental education level, or family income.
- High value should be given to individual family strengths and experiences, including culture and tradition, when creating respectful and trusting relationships between families and professionals who will then share the responsibility for the student's healthy development, learning, and wellness.
- As educational services turn more and more toward a consumer model, parents expect not only effective, consistent, and proactive teacher/parent communication regarding student progress and performance, but also that their ideas, input, and opinions will be heard and responded to.

Chapter 11

Promoting Community Partnerships

Schools and districts are continuously influenced and affected by local and systemic factors that affect how students learn and grow. Extensive collaboration between a wide variety of stakeholders is necessary in order to provide high-quality educational opportunities for students. Collaborations must be intentional, united, and consistent with evidence-based best practices in order to be successful.

The Smart Education System Theory posits that a network of strong, overlapping collaborations between school systems, community organizations, institutes of higher education, and families is essential to transforming education (Annenberg Institute for School Reform, 2015). Collaboration can come in the form of partnerships that are mutually supportive relationships between businesses and school districts and/or schools where the partners obligate themselves to specific goals and activities for the benefit of students and schools (The Council for Corporate & School Partnerships, 2017).

Forming Successful Partnerships

School systems and students consistently have a variety of unmet needs. The formation of P–12/higher education partnerships and school–business partnerships can assist in meeting those needs. Collaborative groups can also enhance and improve student experiences, retention, and success (The Council for Corporate & School Partnerships, 2017). In forming effective partnerships, active communication and feedback should be utilized as the basis for continued improvement, and intervention strategies should be considered and adapted as needed to optimize efficacy (JBL Associates, Inc., 2013).

106   *Chapter 11*

Flexible approaches and an openness to learning will enable partnerships to collaboratively formulate effective and purposeful strategies as necessitated. Written procedures to ensure that processes and activities are reviewed, that outcomes are tracked and measured, and that feedback is openly shared and discussed is important to the long-term success of any partnership (JBL Associates, Inc., 2013).

Collaboration through partnerships with clearly defined roles and responsibilities is more productive when processes and strategies are outlined by achievable goals and are consistent with team members' existing objectives. Partnership goals should be clearly defined, understood by all parties, and based on the needs and desired outcomes of the partners from the outset (JBL Associates, Inc., 2013; The Council for Corporate & School Partnerships, 2017).

Partnerships need to fit in with the norms and values of the community within which the partnership takes place and possess broad stakeholder support (JBL Associates, Inc., 2013). To have a positive impact on students, partnerships should be attuned to the educational goals of the school/district, be consistent with educational policy found at the state and federal levels, and aid in the execution of the requirements set forth in the national education initiative No Child Left Behind (The Council for Corporate & School Partnerships, 2017).

Partnerships between School Districts and Institutes of Higher Education

Institutions of higher education and P–12 schools should strive for a reciprocal partnership in which each offers research capabilities, theoretical knowledge, and instructional strategies to the other (Young & Jean, 2015). With more students striving for a college diploma, P–12 schools can teach colleges and universities strategies to work with a diverse array of students having a wide range of needs and develop strategies to engage families and communities as collaborative partners (Young & Jean, 2015; Annenberg Institute for School Reform, 2015).

Educational coalitions, across city, state, and regional levels, should seek to develop important strategies for aligning expectations across primary, secondary, and postsecondary education; in this way, barriers to access can be removed and students may be better prepared to enter higher education (Annenberg Institute for School Reform, 2015). According to the Annenberg Institute for School Reform (2015), there are several steps that can help school systems and institutes of higher education form effective partnerships that are grounded in community engagement.

Promoting Community Partnerships

- Partners should demonstrate mutual respect for the other's experience, credibility, knowledge, and commitment. Partners should also promise to balance each other's priorities and constraints and ensure that the partnership does indeed benefit both parties. To maintain a shared vision, mutual goals should be worked at with optimism, and the achievement of those goals should be approached with flexibility (Annenberg Institute for School Reform, 2015).
- Partners should meet regularly and consistently and have clear, documented roles, responsibilities, and goals. Processes, projects, and outcomes should be continuously assessed and formed into an organized and detailed contract from which the members of the partnership can work (Annenberg Institute for School Reform, 2015).
- Partners should raise and contribute sufficient resources, including adequate funding, to accomplish the partnership goals. Sufficient time should be dedicated by all members to provide expertise in support of partnership goals. Visions and goals should be sustainable, guide strategic planning, strengthen the collaborative process, and allow time to build and maintain interpersonal trust and relationships between school systems and higher education staff/faculty.
- Partners should be encouraged to broaden faculty, staff, and stakeholder participation and increase opportunities to learn about and engage in partnership. Stakeholders should be invited to learn about and participate in the partnership as well as provide feedback on established goals and activities (Annenberg Institute for School Reform, 2015).
- Community members and organizations should be given the opportunity to learn about and engage in a P–12/higher education partnership. Feedback on the partnership itself and any associated goals should be welcomed, while engagement in activities should strongly be encouraged (Annenberg Institute for School Reform, 2015).
- Partnerships should maintain high visibility across both P–12 and higher education keeping in mind each other's culture and context and being respectful of differing viewpoints and priorities (Annenberg Institute for School Reform, 2015).

The Gap between P–12 and Higher Education

There is a tremendous need for collaboration between P–12 schools and postsecondary institutions. Programs such as the Adopt-A-Classroom project address the need for better university faculty involvement in public schools and provide opportunities for collaboration between P–12 and higher education faculty (Smith et al., 2016).

Smith et al. (2016) contend that the gap between P–12 and higher education has broadened, as college preparation has not necessarily been the primary focus of high schools. Yet, across the country, education as a whole is pushing for the implementation of college and career readiness standards for P–12 schools. Districts are now reaching out to institutes of higher education to assist in enhancing teacher content knowledge (Young & Jean, 2015). Through partnerships with schools, higher education faculty are able to provide not only expertise in particular areas of focus but access to tangible resources as well (Young & Jean, 2015; Smith et al., 2016).

Typically, P–12 and postsecondary institutions exist and operate independently of each other, and partnerships between the two often result in only one side of the partnership actually benefiting, furthering the divide between universities and P–12 teachers (Smith et al., 2016). This division has proven to be problematic for all students, especially those who are underrepresented in higher education (Smith et al., 2016).

The weak connection between P–12 schools and higher education creates a lack of knowledge by schools about what is required in preparing students for college success and a lack of understanding by colleges of the challenges educators at the secondary level face (Smith et al., 2016). To close the gap, P–12 and higher education faculty should be given more opportunities to interact on a consistent basis, especially outside of the teacher education faculty partnership (Smith et al., 2016).

As tenured professors are obligated to perform service as one of the three components in their triad—scholarship, teaching, and service—weaving together these partnerships should not be difficult (Young, Jean, & Quayson, 2018). Forming collaborative partnerships provides an avenue for college faculty to offer current content knowledge and share information about resources in their respective fields, while P–12 teachers can offer insight into current school practices. The connections also teach P–12 students about higher education and give them greater access to and understanding of postsecondary options (Young & Jean, 2015; Young, Jean, & Quayson, 2018; Smith et al., 2016).

College Readiness

School partnerships with higher education can lead to positive impacts, such as professional educator growth, access to real-world connections and resources, and an increase in student motivation to work toward a future in college (Smith et al., 2016). Alignment and collaboration between P–12 and higher education can increase student success not only in achieving college and career readiness but in persisting in and completing college, as well (Young, Jean, & Quayson, 2018; DeMaria et al., 2015).

Promoting Community Partnerships 109

It has been demonstrated that many students who are not fully prepared for college and are required to take at least one remedial course in college do not persist to the second year (Young, Jean, & Quayson, 2018). More than 70 percent of these students will never earn a college degree, and those who do require more time to complete coursework (DeMaria et al., 2015).

In schools where there is an alignment and partnership with institutions of higher education, students have an understanding of what they are required to know and be able to do before graduating high school and entering college. An increase in the number of fully prepared students entering college translates into a higher percentage of students persisting to a college degree in less time and at a lower cost (DeMaria et al., 2015).

P–12/higher education partnerships benefit not only educators but also students and their families. When students enter college and are ready to learn, progress is made much more quickly, the amount of unproductive time and effort is reduced, and students graduate having spent less money with less debt (Young, Jean, & Quayson, 2018; DeMaria et al., 2015).

To be successful, collaborative P–12/higher education partnerships should establish a clear, shared definition of college readiness that includes speci-fied college standards in key academic content areas (DeMaria et al., 2015). For institutions, a strong, focused, and aligned college readiness and college success plan translates into higher enrollments, improved retention, and improved rates of completion (Young, Jean, & Quayson, 2018).

Collaborative initiatives between P–12 and higher education can result in improved academic success and student outcomes, as evidenced by lower dropout rates, increased student preparedness for college, and higher test scores (Young, Jean, & Quayson, 2018; DeMaria et al., 2015). Students who are more prepared for college show positive outcomes and improved statistics for the college such as higher first-year success rates, increased retention rates, more on-time graduations, and increased graduation rates (Young, Jean, & Quayson, 2018; DeMaria et al., 2015).

Many postsecondary institutions are shifting and aligning policies for ad-mission, course placement, and remediation to reflect new assessments and statewide definitions of college readiness. To reach the goal of reducing, if not eliminating, remediation efforts and improving retention and successful outcomes, effectively communicating any policy changes to educators, students, and parents is important (DeMaria et al., 2015).

To ensure that high school students are on track and ready to attend college, schools and higher education institutions should collaborate in the design and deliverance of transition courses. At the state level, dual enrollment strategies and programs like Advanced Placement and International Baccalaureate can be implemented to further support a student's goals in becoming ready for college (Young, Jean, & Quayson, 2018; Young & Jean, 2015; DeMaria et al., 2016).

Postsecondary partners can help P–12 educators to align curriculum, teacher preparation programs, and professional development options to the expectations of new standards and policies. Alignment requires collaboration, and collaboration requires fully engaged partners. With both school and higher education partners committing to the implementation of a shared set of goals and outcomes around college readiness, students are more likely to attend college, remain in college, and become successful in their academic pursuits.

Partnerships between School Districts and Community Businesses

To work as an effective, successful team, school–business partnerships must ratify a set of shared interests and goals attained through shared vision, incorporate mutual benefits, and concretely establish the commitment of each partner to the collaborative process and the ultimate goal of student success (Young & Jean, 2015; JBL Associates, Inc., 2013). To generate measurable outcomes for student success, school-business partnerships rely on communication, contribution, and collaboration of all members and must be purpose-driven and results-oriented (JBL Associates, Inc., 2013).

Partnerships benefit the most when members are open to understanding the cultural values brought into the relationship and guided by trust and mutual respect. Businesses should strive to understand that business culture is different from that found in a school system and that schools operate under different challenges and constraints than businesses (JBL Associates, Inc., 2013). For their part, school systems should be sensitive to the business climate and culture and understand that businesses are guided in operation by a set of norms and assumptions different from what is found within education (JBL Associates, Inc., 2013).

Successful school–business relationships with maximum involvement at the local level can have a powerful impact on the community. Although these partnerships typically involve community members and parents of children in the local school system, their success ultimately benefits the entire community. Schools are widely recognized focal points of any community, and community leaders should be engaged and supportive of school–business partnerships that will improve the educational experiences for all students (The Council for Corporate & School Partnerships, 2017).

While all partnerships strive to attain what is best for students, a majority of successful relationships provide mutual benefits for the school and business partners. Education–business partnerships, for example, have consistently demonstrated value in communities nationwide by providing work-based learning experiences, in addition to funding and equipment to modernize classrooms, workspaces, and labs (JBL Associates, Inc., 2013).

With community partnerships in place, schools have access to mentors, products, funding, and assistance that they might not typically have in preparing students for higher education and the job market. At the same time, by partnering with schools, businesses are able to strengthen connections with students, schools, and communities, thereby strengthening the academic and professional capabilities of future employees (The Council for Corporate & School Partnerships, 2017).

School–business partnerships are highly successful when communities value partnership contributions. To ensure the partnership will be of importance, all relevant parties should be informed of the partnership and have an equal opportunity to discuss the pros and cons as well as provide feedback (The Council for Corporate & School Partnerships, 2017). Schools may want to establish an accountability committee to review the partnership, its impact on students, and whether the students are, indeed, the ultimate beneficiaries of the partnerships (The Council for Corporate & School Partnerships, 2017).

Collaborative working relationships between education and business that are built on a system of shared values and goals can have a significant impact on the effectiveness of educators and on individual student outcomes (JBL Associates, Inc., 2013). Partnership activities involving interaction between students, school staff, business employees, and the community promote learning and offer students valuable experience for their future in the workforce (The Council for Corporate & School Partnerships, 2017).

Education–business partnerships also provide the ability for schools to build success-oriented college and career cultures that empower students and the opportunity for the creation of environments in which students are able to build meaningful relationships with strong role models and mentors (JBL Associates, Inc., 2013).

Business community members are expertly situated to facilitate knowledge and professional skill development among educators by connecting teachers to applied research in their instructional areas and providing opportunities for skill enhancement through mentoring, externships, and job shadowing (JBL Associates, Inc., 2013). Business professionals can directly mentor and coach students to strengthen their comprehension of college and career expectations and develop competence in the skills and qualities needed to be successful in both college and the workforce (JBL Associates, Inc., 2013).

Community business leaders also have specific areas of expertise that may help students focus on long-term goals and objectives and help educators improve curriculum and educational services to be in alignment with and more relevant to student goals (JBL Associates, Inc., 2013). Businesses, for example, can serve as advisors to educators to develop a palpable definition of college readiness, and to aid in the design of instructional frameworks and academic standards and student assessment tools to ensure real-world learning needs are addressed and aligned with the appropriate standards and competencies (JBL Associates, Inc., 2013).

Parental Partnership Roles

Parents can be seen as silent partners in the school–business partner relationship. Parents, along with other members of the community, are key participants in making the partnership a success and help support efforts that undoubtedly benefit schools and community businesses. As such, it is imperative that parents are informed of any school partnerships and are allowed to participate and provide feedback when appropriate (The Council for Corporate & School Partnerships, 2017).

Community Schools

Partnering schools with other organizations will ensure that focus is given to students' developmental and health needs so that they are fully prepared for learning. Many school districts have adopted the idea of creating community schools. Community schools are partnerships among schools, families, and the local community with a focus on supporting student development, educational outcomes, and families, and developing strong communities (West Virginia Department of Education, 2015).

Strong partnerships among schools and service providers enable community schools to deliver integrated approaches to student and family development while providing a path to meet students' nonacademic needs (West Virginia Department of Education, 2015). Student success is supported by actively supporting academic development through the coordination and alignment of programs and outcomes with classroom learning (West Virginia Department of Education, 2015). Community schools are places comprised of partnerships with various community resources, and, as such, their integrated focus on academics, student health, and community development and community engagement leads to improved student learning, stronger families, and healthier communities (West Virginia Department of Education, 2015).

Community schools view the student holistically and offer personalized opportunities and supports designed to remove barriers that prevent students from learning and foster positive attitudes toward learning (West Virginia Department of Education, 2015). Respectful, inclusive school communities, with policies and programs that reflect the diversity of the students and the community, provide a safe environment for students to explore various

Promoting Community Partnerships

interests and grow into highly skilled, creative, and well-rounded adults (West Virginia Department of Education, 2015).

Positive impacts on students, schools, families, and communities include improvement in student learning and attendance, increased participation of parents in student education, and increased opportunities for families to contribute to education and the community (West Virginia Department of Education, 2015). Community schools can empower families and are able to consistently sustain increased parent participation in the success of students by providing a variety of supports.

Poverty, family circumstances, and limited access to medical services may have a substantial impact on a student's ability to successfully learn and develop. Low academic achievement, often found in economically disadvantaged communities, typically leads to numerous challenges that substantially burden community resources (JBL Associates, Inc., 2013).

With a clear focus on health and social supports, community schools are able to utilize existing professional support services, such as school nursing and counseling, to offer families the support they need on a consistent basis (West Virginia Department of Education, 2015). When families are supported and involved, students are more likely to be successful in the classroom, and supportive neighborhoods and available resources are more likely to be sustained (JBL Associates, Inc., 2013).

Community schools recognize and understand that family engagement is crucial to students' success and well-being. To promote family engagement, schools work hard to develop school environments that are welcoming to students, families, and the local community (West Virginia Department of Education, 2015). Effective communication is of the utmost importance, and developing two-way, meaningful communication between school and home using a variety of methods is essential to the sharing of information regarding student achievement, as well as the challenges to student learning (West Virginia Department of Education, 2015).

FINAL THOUGHTS

Mutually supportive and collaborative relationships between schools and higher education, as well as schools and businesses, should have specific goals and outcomes that work toward the benefit of helping students become successful. School systems and students continuously contain a changing set of unmet needs, and the formation of P–12/higher education partnerships and school–business partnerships to help meet those needs will enhance and improve student experiences, retention, and success.

The ever-growing disconnect between P–12 schools and postsecondary institutions demonstrates a tremendous need for collaboration and mutually beneficial relationships to maintain effective research, knowledge bases, and up-to-date instructional strategies. Forming collaborative partnerships provides the opportunity for educators to offer current content knowledge and share information about resources in their respective fields.

School partnerships with higher education will lead to positive impacts for both educators and students, such as professional educator growth, access to a variety of resources, and an increase in student motivation to attend and succeed in college. Collaborative initiatives between stakeholders will result in improved academic success and student outcomes as evidenced by lower dropout rates, increased student preparedness for college, higher first-year college success rates, increased retention rates, and increased graduation rates.

School systems are highly recognized focal points of any community, and community leaders and local businesses should be engaged and supportive of partnerships that seek to improve educational experiences for all students. More and more community-based schools are being established nationwide, with an integrated focus on academics, student health, and community development. Robust community engagement not only will make the community itself resilient, but it will improve student learning, as well as create stronger families and healthier communities overall.

POINTS TO REMEMBER

- Collaboration in any partnership must be intentional, united, and consistent with evidence-based best practices in order to be successful. A network of strong, overlapping alliances between school systems, community organizations, institutes of higher education, and families is essential to transforming education.
- Partnership goals should be clearly defined, understood by all parties, and based on partner needs and desired outcomes. Higher education and business partners should be attuned to the educational goals of P–12 schools and aid in the execution of the requirements set forth in national and state education initiatives.
- Successful school–business relationships with maximum local involvement from community members, parents, and students can have a powerful impact on the community as a whole.
- Effective and meaningful relationships between education and business that are built on a system of shared values and goals will have a

Promoting Community Partnerships

significant impact on the effectiveness of educators and on individual student outcomes.

- Fostering success-oriented college and career environments and cultures that seek to empower students and provide the opportunity for students to build meaningful relationships with strong role models and mentors will help ensure that students succeed not only academically but also in the workforce after graduation.

References

Afterschool Alliance. (2017). *21st-century community learning centers: Providing local afterschool and summer learning programs for families.* Retrieved from http://www.afterschoolalliance.org/policy21stcclc.cfm.

Agrawal, J., & Morin, L.L. (2016). Evidence-Based Practices: Applications of Concrete Representational Abstract Framework across Math Concepts for Students with Mathematics Disabilities. *Learning Disabilities Research & Practice (Wiley-Blackwell), 31*(1), 34–44. doi:10.1111/ldrp.12093.

Akash, C. (2014). *Fighting back against teachers' unions: Saving education in America.* Retrieved from http://www.theblaze.com/contributions/fighting-back-against-teachers-unions-saving-education-in-america/.

Alber, R. (2015). *5 Highly Effective Teaching Practices.* Retrieved from https://www.edutopia.org/blog/5-highly-effective-teaching-practices-rebecca-alber.

Allen-Heath, M., Smith, K., & Young, E. (2017). Using children's literature to strengthen social and emotional learning. *School Psychology International, 38*(5), 541–61. doi:10.11777/0143034317710070.

Animoto. (2017). *Engage students and parents with video.* Retrieved from https://animoto.com/business/education.

Annenberg Institute for School Reform. (2015). *The higher education–district partnership self-assessment rubric: An indicator tool and lessons from Rhode Island College and Central Falls, Rhode Island.* Retrieved from http://www.annenberginstitute.org/sites/default/files/product/814/files/HigherEducationRubric.pdf.

Anrig, G. (2014). Cultivating collaboration: The science behind thriving labor management relationships. *American Federation of Teachers.* Retrieved from https://www.aft.org/periodical/american-educator/winter-2013-2014/cultivating-collaboration.

Anrig, G. (2015). Improving school: What works? *Educational Leadership, 72*(5), 30–35. Retrieved from http://www.ascd.org/publications/educational-leadership/feb15/vol72/num05/How-We-Know-Collaboration-Works.aspx.

Antonucci, M. (2015). Teachers unions and the war within. *EducationNext, (15)*1. Retrieved from http://educationnext.org/teachers-unions-war-within/.

Appleby, M. (2015). *What are the benefits of interdisciplinary study?* Retrieved from http://www.open.edu/openlearn/education/what-are-the-benefits-interdisciplinary-study.

Archer, A., & Hughes, C. (2011). *Explicit instruction: Effective and efficient teaching.* The Guilford Press.

ASCD. (2017). *ESSA and Accountability: Frequently Asked Questions.* Retrieved from http://www.ascd.org/ASCD/pdf/siteASCD/policy/ESSA-Accountability-FAQ_May112016.pdf.

Beauchemin, J., Hutchins, T., & Patterson, F. (2008). Mindfulness meditation may lessen anxiety, promote social skills, and improve academic performance among adolescents with learning disabilities. *Complementary Health Practice Review, 13*(1), 35–45. Retrieved from https://www.researchgate.net/publication/244918853_Mindfulness_Meditation_May_Lessen_Anxiety_Promote_Social_Skills_and_Improve_Academic_Performance_Among_Adolescents_With_Learning_Disabilities.

Bhagi, U. (2017). *12 reasons why project-based learning is better than traditional classroom learning.* Retrieved from https://elearningindustry.com/project-based-learning-better-traditional-classroom.

Bienia, E.J. (2016). *Preschool partnerships: How teachers make sense of their experiences* (doctoral dissertation). Northeastern University. Retrieved from ProQuest.

Bjorn, P., Aro, M., Koponen, T., Fuchs, L., & Fuchs, D. (2016). The many faces of special education within the RTI frameworks in the United States and Finland. *Learning Disabilities Quarterly, 39*(1), 58–66. Retrieved from http://journals.sagepub.com/doi/10.1177/0731948715594787.

Blad, E. (2017). ESSA Law Broadens Definition of School Success. *Education Week, 35*(15), 15. Retrieved from http://www.edweek.org/ew/articles/2016/01/06/essa-law-broadens-definition-of-school-success.html.

Boren, D. (2017). Synergistic school leadership: Coaching teachers, teams, and team leaders. *Leadership, 46*(5), 40–43. Retrieved from http://web.b.ebscohost.com.ezproxy.springfield.edu/ehost/pdfviewer/pdfviewer?vid=1&sid=706450c5-f34c-450f-9644-3a20016b5c0b%40sessionmgr103.

Bowe, J., & Gore, J. (2017). Reassembling teacher professional development: The case for quality teaching rounds. *Teachers and Teaching: Theory & Practice.* doi: 10.1080/13540602.2016.1206522.

Brown, G. (2016). Leadership's influence: A case study of an elementary principal's indirect impact on student achievement. *Education, 137*(1), 101–15. Retrieved from http://web.a.ebscohost.com.ezproxy.springfield.edu/ehost/pdfviewer/pdfviewer?vid=1&sid=dfeda1c0-1265-4a44-84f8-2539674cb669%40sessionmgr4008.

Bubb, S. (2013). Developing from within: Towards a new model of staff development. *Professional Development Today, 15*(1), 13–19. Retrieved from http://connection.ebscohost.com/c/articles/85830135/developing-from-within-towardsnew-model-staff-development.

References

Cannon, J., Jacknowitz, A., & Painter, G. (2011). The effect of attending full-day kindergarten on English language learners. *Journal of Policy Analysis and Management, 30*(2), 287–309. doi:10.1002/pam.20560.

Carnegie Mellon University. (2015). Assessing prior knowledge. *Eberly Center: Teaching Excellence & Educational Innovation.* Retrieved from https://www.cmu.edu/teaching/designteach/teach/priorknowledge.html.

Carroll, T., Fulton, K., & Doerr, H. (2010). Team up for 21st-century teaching and learning: What research and practice reveal about professional learning. *National Commission on Teaching and America's Future. Washington, D.C.* Retrieved from http://files.eric.ed.gov/fulltext/ED512177.pdf.

Centers for Disease Control. (2016). Youth risk behavior surveillance—United States, 2015. *Morbidity and Mortality Weekly Report: Surveillance and Summaries, 65*(6), 1–174. Retrieved from https://www.cdc.gov/mmwr/volumes/65/ss/ss6506a1.htm.

Cho, S., & Cicchelli, T. (2012). Pre-service teachers' multicultural attitudes: Urban and suburban field contexts. *Teacher Education and Practice, 25*(1), 68–76. ISSN: 08906459.

City, E., Elmore, R., Fiarman, S., & Teitel, L. (2010). *Instructional rounds in education: A network approach to improving teaching and learning.* Cambridge, MA: Harvard Education.

Ciullo, S., Falcomata, T. Pfannenstiel, K., & Billingsley, G. (2015). Improving learning with science and social studies text using computer-based concept maps for students with disabilities. *Behavior Modification, 39*(1), 117–35. Retrieved from https://www.researchgate.net/publication/266672926_Improving_Learning_With_Science_and_Social_Studies_Text_Using_Computer-Based_Concept_Maps_for_Students_With_Disabilities.

Collaborative for Academic, Social and Emotional Learning. (2017). *What is SEL?* Retrieved from http://www.casel.org/what-is-sel/.

Colwell, C., MacIsaac, D., Tichenor, M., Heins, B., & Piechura, K. (2014). District and university perspectives on sustaining professional development schools: Do the NCATE standards matter? *The Professional Educator, 38*(2). Retrieved from https://eric.ed.gov/?id=EJ1048336.

Committee for Children. (2017). *Finding lifelong success with social-emotional learning.* Retrieved from http://www.cfchildren.org/programs/social-emotional-learning/.

Committee for Children. (2017a). Bullying Prevention. Retrieved from http://www.cfchildren.org/programs/bullying-prevention/.

Community Schools Network. (2017). *How to engage families to improve student outcomes.* Retrieved from http://www.cacommunityschools.org/how-to-engage-families-to-improve-student-outcomes/.

Connelly, V., & Dockrell, J. (2016). Writing development and instruction for students with learning disabilities. In MacArthur, C., Graham, S., and Fitzgerald, J. (eds.), *Handbook of writing research* (211–26). New York: The Guilford Press.

Council for Exceptional Children. (2014). *CEC releases evidence-based practice standards.* Retrieved from http://www.cec.sped.org/~/media/Files/Standards/Evidence%20based% 20Practices%20and%20Practice/CEC%20Evidence%20Based%20Practice%20News%20Release.pdf.

Council for Exceptional Children. (2008). *Policy Manual*, *4*(3), 1–10. Retrieved from http://www.cec.sped.org/~/media/Files/Policy/CEC%20Professional%20 Policies%20and%20Positions/RTI.pdf.

Council for Exceptional Children. (2014). *Standards for evidence-based practices in special education.* Retrieved from http://www.cec.sped.org/~/media/Files/ Standards/Evidence%20 based%20Practices%20and%20Practice/EBP%20 FINAL.pdf.

Darling-Hammond, L., Willhoit, G., & Pittenger, L. (2014). Accountability for college and career readiness: Developing a new paradigm. *Education Policy Analysis Archives*, *22*(8), 1–38. doi:10.14507/eppa.v.22n86.2014.

Davies, L. (n.d.). *Using bibliotherapy with children.* Retrieved from http://www. kellybear.com/TeacherArticles/TeacherTip34.html.

DeMaria, P., Vaishnav, A., Cristol, K., & Mann, S.B. (2015). *Achieving the Benefits of K–12/Higher Education Alignment.* Retrieved from http://education-first.com/ wp-content/uploads/2015/10/01-Higher-Ed-Alignment-Brief-Intro1.pdf.

DeMonte, J. (2013). *High-quality professional development for teachers: Supporting teacher training to improve student learning.* Retrieved from https://www.americanprogress.org/wp-content/uploads/2013/07/ DeMonteLearning4Teachers-1.pdf.

Desilver, D. (2017). *U.S. students' academic achievement still lags that of their peers in many other countries.* Retrieved from http://www.pewresearch.org/ fact-tank/2017/02/15/u-s-students-internationally-math-science/.

Desimone, L.M., & Pak, K. (2017). *Instructional coaching as high-quality professional development.* doi:10.1080/00405841.2016.1241947.

Diament, M. (2016). Graduation rates lagging for students with disabilities. *Disability Scoop.* Retrieved from https://www.disabilityscoop.com/2016/01/22/ graduation-rates-lagging/21815/.

DoSomething.Org. (n.d.). *11 facts about high school dropout rates.* Retrieved from https://www.dosomething.org/us/facts/11-facts-about-high-school-dropout-rates.

Durlak, J., Dymnicki, A., Taylor, R., Weissberg, R., & Schellinger, K. (2011). The impact of enhancing students' social and emotional learning: A meta-analysis of school based universal interventions. *Child Development*, *82*, 405–32. Retrieved from https://www.researchgate.net/publication/49807966_The_Impact_of_Enhancing_ Students%27_Social_and_Emotional_Learning_A_Meta-Analysis_of_School-Based_Universal_Interventions.

Earley, P., & Porritt, V. (2014). Evaluating the impact of professional development: The need for a student-focused approach. *Professional Development in Education*, *40*(1), 112–29. doi:10.1080/19415257.2013.798741.

Ed Data Express. (2016). Cohort count for regulatory adjusted cohort graduation rate, limited English proficient: 2014–2015. *ED Data Express.* Retrieved from https:// eddataexpress.ed.gov/data-element-explorer.cfm.

Education Commission of the States. (2014). What ELL training, if any, is required of general education teachers. *50 State Comparison.* Retrieved from http://ecs.force. com/mbdata/mbquestNB2?rep=ELL1415.

References

Educators of America. (2017). *What is project-based learning?* Retrieved from https://www.educatorsusa.org/project-based-learning.

Espelage, D., Rose, C., & Polanin, J. (2016). Social emotional learning program to promote prosocial and academic skills among middle school students with disabilities. *Remedial and Special Education, 37*(6), 323–32. Retrieved from http://journals.sagepub.com/doi/abs/10.1177/0741932515627475.

Estrella-Henderson, L., & Jessop, S. (2015). Leadership coaching to close the achievement gap. *Leadership; Association of California School Administrators, 44*(4), 32–6. Retrieved from http://web.b.ebscohost.com.ezproxy.springfield.edu/ehost/pdfviewer/pdfviewer?vid=1&sid=8e51199a-2a17-43da-9bf1-43c4bb45656d%40sessionmgr4009.

Fenner, D. (2013). Implementing the common core state standards for English language learners: The changing role of the ESL teacher. *TESOL International Association.* Retrieved from http://www.tesol.org/docs/default-source/advocacy/ccss_convening_final-8-15-13.pdf?sfvrsn=8.

Ficarra, L., & Quinn, K. (2014). Teachers' facility with evidence-based classroom management practices: An investigation of teacher preparation programs and in-service conditions. *Journal of Teacher Education for Sustainability, 16*(2), 71–87. Retrieved from http://files.eric.ed.gov/fulltext/EJ1108117.pdf.

Flanagan, S., & Bouck, E. (2015). Mapping out the details: Supporting struggling writers' written expression with concept mapping. *Preventing School Failure, 59*(4). 244–52.

Flores, M., Hinton, V., Strozier, S., & Terry, S. (2014). Using the concrete-representational-abstract sequence and the strategic instruction model to teach computation to teach students with autism spectrum disorders and developmental disabilities. *Education and Training in Autism and Developmental Disabilities, 49*(4), 547–54. Retrieved from http://daddcec.org/Portals/0/ETADD49(4)_547-554.pdf.

Ford, J. (2013). *Educating students with learning disabilities.* Retrieved from http://corescholar.libraries.wright.edu/cgi/viewcontent.cgi?article=1154&context=ejie.

Friedberg, R., Hoyman, L., Behar, S., Tabbarah, S., Pacholec, N., Keller, M., & Thordarson, M. (2014). We've come a long way, baby! Evolution and revolution in CBT with youth. *Journal of Rational-Emotive & Cognitive Behavior Therapy, 32*, 4–14. doi:10.1007/s10942-014-0178-3.

Fuchs, D., Fuchs, L., & Compton, D. (2012). Smart RTI: A next generation approach to multilevel prevention. *Exceptional Children, 78*, 263–79. Retrieved from journals.sagepub.com/doi/abs/10.1177/001440291207800301?patientinform-links=yesl78%2F3%2F263r78%2F3%2F263c78%2F3%2F263c78%2F3%2F263r78%2F3%2F263.

Fuchs, D., Fuchs, L., & Stecker, P. (2010). The blurring of special education in a new continuum of general education placements and services. *Exceptional Children, 76*, 301–23. Retrieved from http://journals.sagepub.com/doi/abs/10.1177/001440291007600304.

Gabriel, J., & Farmer, P. (2009). Developing a vision and mission. In *How to help your school thrive without breaking the bank*. ASCD. Retrieved from http://www.

ascd.org/publications/books/107042/chapters/Developing-a-Vision-and-a-Mission.
aspx.

Garcia, P., & Morales, P. (2016). Exploring quality programs for English language learners in charter schools: A framework to guide future research. *Education Policy Analysis Archives*, *24*(53). Retrieved from http://dx.doi.org/10.14507/epaa.24.1739.

Geeraerts, K., Tynjala, P., Heikkinen, H., Markkanen, I., Pennanen, M., & Gijbels, D. (2015). Peer-group mentoring as a toll for teacher development. *European Journal of Teacher Education*. doi:10.1080/19415257.2013.798741.

Gibbs, C. (2013). Reconciling experimental and quasi-experimental evidence on the impact of full-day kindergarten. *Society for Research and Educational Effectiveness*. Retrieved from https://eric.ed.gov/?q=kansas+full+day+kindergarten&id=ED564096.

Glass, K. (2017). *7 strategies for using context clues in reading*. Retrieved from https://www.teachthought.com/literacy/7-strategies-using-context-clues-reading/.

Glende, L. (2013). *Vocabulary and word study to increase comprehension in content areas for struggling readers*. Retrieved from http://fisherpub.sjfc.edu/cgi/viewcontent.cgi?article=1248&context=education_ETD_masters.

Grant, K.B., & Ray, J.A. (2015). *Home, school, and community collaboration: Culturally responsive family engagement* (3rd ed.). Thousand Oaks, CA: Sage.

Green, T., & Allen, M. (2015). Professional development urban schools: What do teachers say? *Journal of Inquiry and Action in Education*, *6*(2), 53–6. Retrieved from http://digitalcommons.buffalostate.edu/jiae/vol6/iss2/5/.

Gueldner, B., & Feuerborn, L. (2016). Integrating mindfulness-based practices into social and emotional learning: A case application. *Mindfulness*, *7*, 164–75. Retrieved from https://www.researchgate.net/publication/281234192_Integrating_Mindfulness-based_Practices_into_Social_and_Emotional_Learning_a_Case_Application.

Hall, C. (2015). Inference instruction for struggling readers: A synthesis of intervention research. *Educational Psychology Review*. New York: Springer Science Business Media.

Hamilton, L.S. (2017). *Teachers Matter: Understanding Teachers' Impact on Student Achievement*. Retrieved from https://www.rand.org/education/projects/measuring-teacher-effectiveness/teachers-matter.html.

Harris, K., & Graham, S. (2013). An adjective is a word hanging down from a noun: Learning to write and students with learning disabilities. *Annals of Dyslexia*, *63*, 65–79.

Heckman, P.E., & Sanger, C. (2013). *Expanding minds and opportunities: Leveraging the power of afterschool and summer learning for student success*. Retrieved from http://www.expandinglearning.org/sites/default/files/em_articles/1_howqualityafterschool.pdf.

Hoover, J., & Sarris, J. (2014). Six essential instructional roles to implement response to intervention models: Perceptions of highly qualified special educators. *American Journal of Educational Research*, *2*(5), 257–66. doi:10.12691/education-2-5-4.

References

Hoppey, D. (2013). Linking action research to response to intervention (RtI): The strategy implementation project. *Networks: An online journal for teacher research, 15*(1), 1–10. Retrieved from http://journals.library.wisc.edu/index.php/networks/article/viewFile/624/625.

Hughes, E.M., Powell, S.R., Lembke, E.S., & Riley-Tillman, T.C. (2016). Taking the Guesswork out of Locating Evidence-Based Mathematics Practices for Diverse Learners. *Learning Disabilities Research & Practice (Wiley-Blackwell), 31*(3), 130–41. doi:10.1111/ldrp.12103.

Hurlbut, A., & Tunks, J. (2016). Elementary preservice teachers' experiences with response to intervention. *Teacher Education Qu.arterly.* Summer 2016, 25–48. Retrieved from http://files.eric.ed.gov/fulltext/EJ1110288.pdf

Individuals with Disabilities Education Improvement Act. 34 CFR§612.8(c)(10), 2004.

JBL Associates, Inc. (2013). *Business Engagement in Education: Key Partners for Improving Student Success.* Retrieved from https://www.amgenbiotechexperience.com/sites/default/files/business_engagement_ed_es_0.pdf.

Johnson, D. (2015). The responsive staff meeting. *Educational Leadership, 72*(4). Retrieved from http://www.ascd.org/publications/educational-leadership/dec14/vol72/num04/The-Responsive-Staff-Meeting.aspx.

Johnson, T., & Wells, L. (2017). English language learner teacher effectiveness and the common core. *Education Policy Analysis Archives, 25*(23). ISSN: 1068-2341. Retrieved from http://epaa.asu.edu/ojs/article/view/2395.

K12 Academics. (2017). *Interdisciplinary teaching.* Retrieved from http://www.k12academics.com/interdisciplinary-teaching#.WdrDBGhSxPY.

Kaldenberg, E., Watt, S., & Therrien, W. (2014). Reading instruction in science for students with learning disabilities: A meta-analysis. *Learning Disabilities Quarterly, 38*(3), 160–73.

Kang, E.Y., McKenna, J., Arden, S., & Ciullo, S. (2015). Integrated reading and writing interventions for students with learning disabilities: A review of the literature. *Learning Disabilities Research & Practice, 31*(1), 22–33.

Kelly, K. (2014). *Fostering inclusion with universal design for learning.* Retrieved from https://www.aacu.org/diversitydemocracy/2014/fall/kelly.

Kelly, M. (2017). *Eight things teachers can do to help students succeed: Tips on fostering student success.* Retrieved from https://www.thoughtco.com/ways-teachers-can-help-students-succeed-8082.

Kim, W., Linan-Thompson, S., & Misquitta, R. (2012). Critical factors in reading comprehension instruction for students with LD: A research synthesis. *LD Research & Practice, 27*(2), 66–78.

King Thorius, K., & Maxcy, B. (2015). Critical practice analysis of special education policy: An RTI example. *Remedial and Special Education, 36*(2), 116–24. Retrieved from http://journals.sagepub.com/doi/10.1177/0741932514550812.

King Thorius, K., Maxcy, B., Macey, E., & Cox, A. (2014). A critical practice analysis of response to intervention appropriation in an urban school. *Remedial and Special Education, 35*(5), 287–99. doi:10.1177/0741932514522100.

Klein, A. (2015). No child left behind: An overview. *Ed Week*. Retrieved from http://www.edweek.org/ew/section/multimedia/no-child-left-behind-overview-definition-summary.html.

Kochan, T.A., & Bluestone, B. (2015). *Results and research from the first two years.* Retrieved from http://www.renniecenter.org/sites/default/files/media-icons/MEP_Research_FirstTwoYears.pdf.

Krasnoff, B. (2015). *What the research says about class size, professional development, and recruitment, induction, and retention of highly qualified teachers: A compendium of the evidence on Title-II, Part A, program-funded strategies.* Retrieved from http://files.eric.ed.gov/fulltext/ED558138.pdf.

Kuo, N. (2015). Understanding the philosophical foundations of disabilities to maximize the potential of response to intervention. *Edcuational Philosophy and Theory*, *47*(7), 647–60. Retrieved from https://www.researchgate.net/publication/271946164_Understanding_the_Philosophical_Foundations_of_Disabilities_to_Maximize_the_Potential_of_Response_to_Intervention.

Lauer, P., Christopher, D., Firpo-Triplett, R., & Buchting, F. (2014). The impact of short-term professional development on participant outcomes: A review of the literature. *Professional Development in Education*, *40*(2), 207–27. doi:10.1080/19415257.2013.776619.

Lavoie, R. (2017). *The teacher's role in home/school communication: Everybody wins.* Retrieved from http://www.ldonline.org/article/28021.

Leonard, J. (2012). *Changing roles: Special education teachers in a response to intervention model.* Retrieved from http://opencommons.uconn.edu/cgi/viewcontent.cgi?article=1246&context=srhonors_theses.

Lexia. (2016). *Understanding the unique needs of Title I students.* Retrieved from https://www.lexialearning.com/blog/understanding-unique-needs-title-i-students#.

Lum, G. (2017). *Collective bargaining in education.* Retrieved from https://www.accordence.com/resources/articles-tips/articles/collective-bargaining-in-education/.

Maheady, L., Rafferty, L., Patti, A., & Budin, S. (2016). Leveraging change: Influencing the implementation of evidence-based practice to improve outcomes for students with disabilities. *Learning Disabilities: A Contemporary Journal*, *14*(2), 109–20. Retrieved from http://www.ldw-ldcj.org/index.php/open-access-articles/8-testblog/61-leveraging-evidence-based-practices-from-policy-to-action.html.

Malow, M. (2015). Social-emotional development: Learning disabilities and anxiety: Common undesirable partners. *Learning Disabilities Worldwide*, *8*(2). Retrieved from https://www.ldworldwide.org/single-post/2015/01/01/V8-2-Social-Emotional-Development---Learning-Disabilities-and-Anxiety-Common-Undesirable-Partners.

Marrongelle, K., Sztajn, P., & Smith, M. (2013). Scaling up professional development in an era of common core state standards. *Journal of Teacher Education*, *64*(3), 202–18. doi:10.1177/0022487112473838.

Marshall, K., Karvonen, M., Yell, M., Lowry, A., Drasgow, E., & Seaman, M. (2013). Project ReSpecT: Toward an evidence-based mentoring model for induction teachers. *Journal of Disability Policy Studies*, Sage Publications, *24*(3), 127–36. doi:10.1177/1044207313480837.

References

Marzano, R.J., & Toth, M.D. (2014). *Teaching for rigor: A call for a critical instructional shift: Why essential shifts in instruction are necessary for teachers and students to succeed with college and career readiness standards.* Retrieved from http://www.marzanocenter.com/files/Teaching-for-Rigor-20140318.pdf.

Mason-Williams, L., Frederick, J.R., & Mulchay, C.A. (2015). Building adaptive expertise and practice-based evidence: Applying the implementation stages framework to special eduation teacher preparation. *Teacher Education and Special Education, 38*(3), 207–20. Retrieved from http://journals.sagepub.com/doi/10.1177/0888406414551285.

McHatton, P., & Parker, A. (2013). Purposeful preparation: Longitudinally exploring inclusion attitudes of general and special education pre-service teachers. *Teacher Education and Special Education, 36*(3), 186–203. Retrieved from http://journals.sagepub.com/doi/10.1177/0888406413491611.

Mead, A.E. (2017). *Understanding parents school experiences and how it influences their intent to engage with their child's school* (unpublished dissertation). Boston: Northeastern University.

Meiklejohn, J., Phillips, C., Freedman, M., Griffin, M., Biegel, G., Roach, A., & Saltzman, A. (2012). Integrating mindfulness training into K12 education: Fostering the resilience of teachers and students. *Mindfulness, 3*(4), 291–307. Retrieved from http://www.mindful-well-being.com/wp-content/uploads/2014/07/Meiklejohn-et-al-2012.pdf.

Meyer, A., Rose, D., & Gordon, D. (2014). *Universal design for learning: Theory and practice.* Wakefield, MA: CAST.

Milligan, K., Badali, P., & Spiroiu, F. (2015). Using integra mindfulness martial arts to address self-regulation challenges in youth with learning disabilities: A qualitative exploration. *Journal of Child and Family Studies, 24*, 562–75. Retrieved from https://link.springer.com/article/10.1007/s10826-013-9868-1.

Mills, G.E. (2018). *Action research: A guide for the teacher researcher* (6th ed). New York: Pearson.

Ministry of Education and British Columbia School Superintendent's Association (2011). *Supporting students with learning disabilities: A guide for teachers.* Retrieved from http://www.bced.gov.bc.ca/specialed/docs/learning_disabilities_guide.pdf.

Mitchell, B., Deshler, D., & Lenz, B.K. (2012). Examining the role of the special educator in a response to intervention model. *Learning Disabilities: A Contemporary Journal, 10*(2), 53–74. Retrieved from https://eric.ed.gov/?id=EJ998225.

Mitchell, R., Kensler, L., & Tschannen-Moran, M. (2015). Examining the effects of instructional leadership on school academic press and student achievement. *Journal of School Leadership, 25*, 223–51. Retrieved from https://springfieldcollege.on.worldcat.org/oclc/5866743809.

Morin, A. (n.d.). *4 ways kids use self-monitoring to learn.* Retrieved from https://www.understood.org/en/learning-attention-issues/child-learning-disabilities/executive-functioning-issues/4-ways-kids-use-self-monitoring-to-learn.

Nathanson, L., Rives, S., Flynn, L., & Brackett, M. (2016). Creating emotionally intelligent schools with RULER. *Emotion Review*, *8*(4), 305–10. doi:10.1177/1754073916650495.

National Association of School Psychologists. (2016). *Building Capacity for Student Success; Every Student Succeeds Act Opportunities: Overview for School Psychologists*. Retrieved from www.nasponline.org.

National Center for Children in Poverty. (2017). *Addressing the Challenge*. Retrieved from http://www.nccp.org/about.html.

National Center for Education Statistics. (2012). The nation's report card: Writing 2011 (NECES 2012–470). Washington, DC: Institute of Educational Sciences. U.S. Department of Education. Retrieved from https://nces.ed.gov/nationsreportcard/pdf/main2011/2012470.pdf.

National Center for Education Statistics. (2016). *Allocating grants for Title I.* Retrieved from https://nces.ed.gov/surveys/AnnualReports/pdf/titleI20160111.pdf.

National Center for Education Statistics. (2017). The condition of education: Disability rates and employment status by educational attainment. Washington, DC: Institute of Educational Sciences. U.S. Department of Education. Retrieved from https://nces.ed.gov/programs/coe/indicator_tad.asp.

National Center on Response to Intervention. (n.d.). *What is fidelity?* Retrieved from http://www.rti4success.org/sites/default/files/Using%20Fidelity%20to%20Enhance%20Program%20Implementation_PPTSlides.pdf.

National Center on Universal Design for Learning. (2017). *UDL guidelines: Theory and practice.* Retrieved from http://www.udlcenter.org/aboutudl/udlguidelines_theorypractice.

National Education Association. (n.d.). *Full-day kindergarten: An advocacy guide.* Retrieved from http://www.nea.org/assets/docs/HE/mf_kadvoguide.pdf.

National School Boards Association. (2015). *Title I Portability.* Retrieved from https://www.nsba.org/sites/default/files/file/NSBA-Title-I-Portability.pdf.

Obiakor, F., Harris, M., Mutua, K., Rotatori, A., & Algozzine, B. (2012). Making inclusion work in general education classrooms. *Education and Treatment of Children*, *35*, 477–90. Retrieved from https://www.thefreelibrary.com/Making+inclusion+work+in +general+education+classrooms.-a0301649979.

OECD. (2012). *Education at a Glance 2012: OECD Indicators.* Paris: OECD Publishing. Retrieved from http://dx.doi.org/10.1787/eag-2012-en.

Ohio Department of Education. (2016). *Sample best practices for parent involvement in schools.* Retrieved from http://education.ohio.gov/Topics/Other-Resources/Family-and-Community-Engagement/Getting-Parents-Involved/Sample-Best-Practices-for-Parent-Involvement-in-Sc.

Osten, M., & Gidseg, E. The hows and whys of peer mentoring. *Rethinking Schools.* Retrieved from http://rethinkingschools.aidcvt.com/special_reports/quality_teachers/peersd.shtml.

Padilla-Frausto, D., Grant, D., Aydin, H., & Anguilar-Gaxiola, S. (2014). *Three out of four children with mental health needs in California do not receive treatment despite having health care coverage.* Los Angeles: UCLA Center for Health Policy

References

Research. Retrieved from http://healthpolicy.ucla.edu/publications/Documents/PDF /2014/ childmentalhealthbrief-july2014.pdf.

Padron, Y., & Waxman, H. (2016). Investigating principals' knowledge and perceptions of second language programs for English language learners. *International Journal of Educational Leadership and Management, 4*(2), 127–46. doi:10.17583/ijelm.2016,1706.

Parker, E., Diffey, L., & Atchison, B. (2016). Full-day kindergarten: A look across the states. *Education Commission of the States*. Retrieved from http://files.eric.ed.gov/fulltext/ED569133.pdf.

Pellegrino, J., & Hilton, M. (eds.). (2013). Education for life and work: Developing transferable knowledge and skills in the 21st century. *National Academies Press*. Retrieved from https://www.nap.edu/catalog/13398/education-for-life-and-work-developing-transferable-knowledge-and-skills.

Rathbun, A. (2010). Making the most of extra time: Relationships between full-day kindergarten instructional environments and reading achievement. *American Institutes for Research Federal Statistics Program*. Retrieved from http://files.eric.ed.gov/fulltext/ED511350.pdf.

Ravani, G. (2014). *Why public education needs teachers' unions*. Retrieved from https://edsource.org/2014/why-public-education-needs-teachers-unions/65723.

Renard, L. (2017). *30 creative ways to use Padlet for teachers and students*. Retrieved from https://www.bookwidgets.com/blog/2017/08/30-creative-ways-to-use-padlet-for-teachers-and-students.

Rennie Center. (2017). Labor management collaboration. *Massachusetts Education Partnership*. Retrieved from http://www.renniecenter.org/initiatives/labor-management-collaboration.

Rizga, K. (2015). Why so many teachers quit, and how to fix that. *Los Angeles Times*. Retrieved from https://www.theguardian.com/education/2017/jul/08/almost-a-quarter-of-teachers-who-have-qualified-since-2011-have-left-profession.

Rosen, R., & Parise, L. (2017). *Using evaluation systems for teacher improvement: Are school districts ready to meet new federal goals?* Retrieved from https://www.mdrc.org/sites/default/files/iPD_ESSA_Brief_2017.pdf.

Rubinstein, S.A., & McCarthy, J.E. (2014). *Teachers unions and management partnerships: How working together improves student achievement*. Retrieved from https://www.americanprogress.org/issues/education/reports/2014/03/25/86332/teachers-unions-and-management-partnerships/.

Rubinstein, S.A., & McCarthy, J.E. (2016). Union-management partnerships, teacher collaboration, and student performance. *ILR Review*. Retrieved from doi:10.1177/0019793916660508.

Samuels, C.A. (2016). *Number of U.S. students in special education ticks upward*. Retrieved from http://www.edweek.org/ew/articles/2016/04/20/number-of-us-students-in-specialeducation.htmlReferences.

Sansosti, F., Goss, S., & Noltemeyer, A. (2011). Perspectives of special education directors on response to intervention in secondary schools. *Contemporary School Psychology, 15*, 9–20. Retrieved from http://files.eric.ed.gov/fulltext/EJ934702.pdf.

Satsangi, R., & Bouck, E. (2014). Using virtual manipulative instruction to teach the concepts of area and perimeter to secondary students with disabilities. *Learning Disabilities Quarterly, 38*(3), 174–86. doi:10.1177/0731948714550101.

Savage, M. (2017). Almost a quarter of teachers who have qualified have left the profession. *The Guardian.* Retrieved from https://www.theguardian.com/education/2017/jul/08/almost-a-quarter-of-teachers-who-have-qualified-since-2011-have-left-profession.

Scheeler, M., Budin, S., & Markelz, A. (2016). The role of teacher preparation in evidence-based practices in schools. *Learning Disabilities: A Contemporary Journal, 14*(2), 171–87. Retrieved from http://www.ldw-ldcj.org/index.php/open-access-articles/8-testblog/64-the-role-of-teacher-preparation-in-promoting-evidence-based-practice-in-schools.html.

Schmit, S., Matthews, H., & Golden, O. (2014). *Thriving children, successful parents: A two-generation approach to policy.* Retrieved from http://www.clasp.org/resources-and-publications/publication-1/Two-Gen-Brief-FINAL.pdf.

Scruggs, T., Mastropieri, M., & Marshak, L. (2012). Peer-mediated instruction in inclusive secondary social studies learning: Direct and indirect learning effects. *Learning Disabilities Research & Practice, 27,* 12–20. doi:10.111 1/j.1540-5826.2011.00356.

Smith, E., Kindall, H.D., Cartern, V., & Beachner, M. (2016). Impact of adopt-a-classroom partnerships between P-12 and university faculty. *School Community Journal. 26*(1), Retrieved from http://files.eric.ed.gov/fulltext/EJ1104388.pdf.

Solis, M., Vaughn, S., Swanson E., & McCulley, L. (2012). Collaborative models of instruction: The empirical foundation of inclusion and co-teaching. *Psychology in the Schools, 49,* 498–510. Retrieved from http://onlinelibrary.wiley.com/doi/10.1002/pits.21606/abstract.

Stanberry, K. (2016). *What the science says: Effective reading interventions for kids with learning disabilities.* Retrieved from https://www.greatschools.org/gk/articles/effective-reading-interventions/.

Stein, L. (2016). Schools need leaders—not managers: It's time for a paradigm shift. *Journal of Leadership Education, 15*(2), 21–30. doi:1012806/v15/12/13.

Stephens, T.L. (2015). *Encouraging positive student engagement and motiv-ation: Tips for teachers.* Retrieved from http://www.pearsoned.com/education-blog/encouraging-positive-student-engagement-and-motivation-tips-for-teachers/.

Stewart, V. (2012). *A world-class education.* Alexandria, VA: ASCD.

Strickland, T., & Maccinin, P. (2013). The effects of the concrete-representation-abstract integration strategy on the ability of students with learning disabilities to multiply linear expressions within area problems. *Remedial and Special Education, 34*(3), 142–53. doi:10.1177/0741932512441712.

Students Can't Wait. (2015). *Indicators: What to include in school rankings.* Retrieved from https://studentscantwait.org/resource/indicators-include-school-ratings/.

Students Can't Wait. (2015a). *An introduction to school accountability under ESSA.* Retrieved from https://studentscantwait.org/resource/introduction-school-accountability-essa/.

Students Can't Wait. (2015b). *The School Improvement Process: An Overview.* Retrieved from https://studentscantwait.org/resource/school-improvement-process/.

References

Swanson, E., Solis, M., Stephen, C., & McKenna, J. (2012). Special education teachers' perceptions and instructional practices in response to intervention implementation. *Learning Disability Quarterly*, *35*(2), 115–26. Retrieved from http://journals.sagepub.com/doi/abs/10.1177/0731948711432510.

TeacherVision. (2017). *Activating prior knowledge*. Retrieved from https://www.teachervision.com/reading-comprehension/activating-prior-knowledge.

The Council for Corporate & School Partnerships. (2017). *A how-to guide for school-business partnerships*. Retrieved from http://www.nhscholars.org/School-Business%20How_to_Guide.pdf.

The Education Trust. (2014). *School ratings: An overview*. Retrieved from https://edtrust.org/students-cant-wait/school-ratings-2/.

The Nation's Report Card. (n.d.). 2015 Mathematics & reading assessments. Retrieved from https://www.nationsreportcard.gov/reading_math_2015/#?grade=4.

Theoharis, G., & Causton, J. (2014). Leading inclusive school reform for students with disabilities: A school- and system-wide approach. *Theory into Practice*, *53*, 82–97. Retrieved from http://www.tandfonline.com/doi/abs/10.1080/00405841.2014.885808?journalCode=htip20.

Tomlinson, C. (2014). *The differentiated classroom: Responding to the needs of all learners* (2nd ed). Alexandria, VA: ASCD.

Toor, S. (2011). Differentiating leadership from management: An empirical investigation of leaders and managers. *Leadership & Management in Engineering*, *11*(4), 310–20. Retrieved from http://ascelibrary.org/doi/abs/10.1061/%28ASCE%29LM.1943-5630.0000138.

Trites, N. (2017). *What is co-teaching? An introduction to co-teaching and inclusion*. Retrieved from http://castpublishing.org/introduction-co-teaching-inclusion/.

Troia, G., & Olinghouse, N. (2013). The common core state standards and evidence-based educational practices: The case of writing. *School Psychology Review*, *42*(3), 343–57.

U.S. Department of Education. (2015). *Improving basic programs operated by local educational agencies (Title I, Part A)*. Retrieved from https://www2.ed.gov/programs/titleiparta/index.html.

U.S. Department of Education. (2016). *The Every Student Succeeds Act of 2016*. Retrieved from https://www2.ed.gov/policy/elsec/leg/essa/index.html.

U.S. Department of Education. (2017). *21st-century community learning centers*. Retrieved from https://www2.ed.gov/programs/21stcclc/index.html.

U.S. Department of Education. (2017). *Family and Community Engagement*. Retrieved from https://www.ed.gov/parent-and-family-engagement.

U.S. Department of Health and Human Services and U.S. Department of Education Policy. (2016). *Statement on family engagement from the early years to the early grades*. Retrieved from https://www2.ed.gov/about/inits/ed/earlylearning/files/policy-statement.

Vanassche, E., & Kelchtermans, G. (2016). *A narrative analysis of a teacher educator's professional learning journey*. doi:10.1080/02619768.2016.1187127.

Vaughn, S., & Wanzek, J. (2014). Intensive interventions in reading for students with reading disabilities: Meaningful impacts. *LD Research & Practice*, *29*(2), 46–53.

Ventello, G.P. (2017). *The negotiator: Conditions for successful interest-based bargaining*. Retrieved from http://www.nea.org/home/53409.htm.

von Hoene, L. (2017). *Five ways to improve your teaching*. Retrieved from http://gsi.berkeley.edu/gsi-guide-contents/improve-intro/five-ways/.

Watson, S., & Gable, R. (2013). Unraveling the complex nature of mathematics learning disability. Implications for research and practice. *Learning Disability Quarterly, 36*(3), 178–87. doi:10.1177/0731948712461489.

Watson, S., Gable, R., Gear, S., & Hughes, K. (2012). Evidence-based strategies for improving the reading comprehension of secondary students: Implications for students with LD. *LD Research & Practice, 27*(2), 79–89.

Werts, M., & Carpenter, E. (2013). Implementation of tasks in RTI. Perceptions of special education teachers. *Teacher Education and Special Education: The Journal of Teacher Education Division of the Council for Exceptional Children, 3*, 246–57. Retrieved from http://journals.sagepub.com/doi/abs/10.1177/0888406413495420?journalCode=tesa.

West Virginia Department of Education. (2015). *Building community and school partnerships for student success: A resource guide for West Virginia*. Retrieved from http://wvde.state.wv.us/healthyschools/CommunitySchools/CommunitySchoolGuidanceDocumentMarch2015.pdf.

What Works Clearinghouse. (2017). *Scientific evidence*. Retrieved from https://ies.ed.gov/ncee/wwc/WhatWeDo.

Willby, R. (2004). Hiring and retaining high-quality teachers: What principals can do. *Journal of Catholic Education, 8*(2). Retrieved from http://digitalcommons.lmu.edu/cgi/viewcontent.cgi?article=1307&context=ce.

Wilson, D., & Conyers, M. (2017). *Smart strategies for student success: Five techniques you can use with students in any class to help boost their long-term learning outcomes*. Retrieved from https://www.edutopia.org/blog/smart-strategies-student-success-donna-wilson-marcus-conyers.

Wolpert-Gawron, H. (2015). *What the heck is project-based learning?* Retrieved from https://www.edutopia.org/blog/what-heck-project-based-learning-heather-wolpert-gawron.

World Health Organization. (2017). *Child and adolescent mental health*. Retrieved from http://www.who.int/mental_health/maternal-child/child_adolescent/en/.

Young N. D., & Celli, L.M. (2014). *Learning style perspectives: Impact in the classroom* (3rd ed.). Madison, WI: Atwood.

Young, N. D., & Jean, E. (2015a). Educating and Economizing: Innovative K-12/Higher Education Partnerships. In N.D. Young & P. Bittel (eds.), *Educational entrepreneurship: Promoting public-private partnerships for the 21st century*. Lanham, MD: Rowman & Littlefield.

Young, N. D., & Jean, E. (2017). The fundamentals of virtual teaching: Opportunities and Approaches. In N.D. Young & L.M. Celli (eds.), *The power of the professoriate: Demands, challenges, and opportunities in 21st century higher education*. Madison, WI: Atwood.

Young, N. D., & Jean, E. (2018). Parents make the difference: Fostering emotional resiliency to improve school outcomes. In N.D. Young, C.N. Michael, & T.A. Citro

References 131

(eds.), *Emotions and education: Promoting positive mental health in students with learning disabilities*. Wilmington, DE: Vernon.

Young, N. D., Jean, E., & Mead, A.E. (2018). Cultural considerations: Promoting emotional well-being in students with learning disabilities. In N.D. Young, C.N. Michael, & T.A. Citro (eds.), *Emotions and education: Promoting positive mental health in students with learning disabilities*. Wilmington, DE: Vernon.

Young, N. D., Jean, E., & Mead, A.E. (2018a). *From cradle to classroom: Identifying and addressing the needs of our youngest children*. Wilmington, DE: Vernon.

Young, N. D., Jean, E., & Quayson, F.O. (2018). *Lecture hall to laptop: The evolution of virtual education*. Madison, WI: Atwood.

Zenner, C., Hermleben-Kurz, S., & Walach, H. (2014). Mindfulness-based interventions in schools: A systematic review and meta-analysis. *Frontiers in psychology, 5*. Retrieved from http://journal.frontiersin.org/article/10.3389/fpsyg.2014.00603/full.

Zwiers, J. (2015). Every teacher is a language teacher. *Jossey Bass Education*. Retrieved from http://josseybasseducation.com/uncategorized/every-teacher-language-teacher/.

About the Authors

Dr. Nicholas D. Young has worked in diverse educational roles for more than twenty-nine years, serving as a principal, special education director, graduate professor, graduate program director, graduate dean, and longtime superintendent of schools. He was named the Massachusetts Superintendent of the Year, and he completed a distinguished Fulbright program focused on the Japanese educational system through the collegiate level. Dr. Young is the recipient of numerous other honors and recognitions, including the General Douglas MacArthur Award for distinguished civilian and military leadership and the Vice Admiral John T. Hayward Award for exemplary scholarship. He holds several graduate degrees, including a PhD in educational administration and an EdD in educational psychology.

Dr. Young has served in the U.S. Army and the U.S. Army Reserves combined for over thirty-four years, and he graduated with distinction from the U.S. Air War College, the U.S. Army War College, and the U.S. Navy War College. After completing a series of senior leadership assignments in the U.S. Army Reserves as the commanding officer of the 287th Medical Company (DS), the 405th Area Support Company (DS), the 405th Combat Support Hospital, and the 399th Combat Support Hospital, he transitioned to his current military position as a faculty instructor at the U.S. Army War College in Carlisle, Pennsylvania. He currently holds the rank of colonel.

Dr. Young is also a regular presenter at state, national, and international conferences, and he has written many books, book chapters, and articles on various topics in education, counseling, and psychology. Some of his most recent books include *Stars in the Schoolhouse: Teaching Practices and Approaches that Make a Difference* (in-press); *Captivating Classrooms: Student Engagement at the Heart of School Improvement* (in-press); *Guardian of the Next Generation: Igniting the Passion for Quality Teaching* (in-press); *From Head to Heart: High Quality Teaching Practices in the Spotlight* (in-press); *Dog Tags to Diploma: Understanding and Addressing the Educational Needs of Veterans, Servicemembers, and their Families* (in-press); *From Cradle to Classroom: A Guide to Special Education for Young Children* (in-press); *Making the Grade: Promoting Positive Outcomes for Students with Learning Disabilities* (at press); *Paving the Pathway for Educational Success: Effective Classroom Interventions for Students with Learning Disabilities* (at press); *Wrestling with Writing: Effective Strategies for Struggling Students* (at press); *Floundering to Fluent: Reaching and Teaching the Struggling Student* (at press); *Emotions and Education: Promoting Positive Mental Health in Students with Learning Disabilities* (2018); *From Lecture Hall to Laptop: Opportunities, Challenges, and the Continuing Evolution of Virtual Learning in Higher Education* (2017); *The Power of the Professoriate: Demands, Challenges, and Opportunities in 21st-Century Higher Education* (2017); *To Campus with Confidence: Supporting a Successful Transition to College for Students with Learning Disabilities* (2017); *Educational Entrepreneurship: Promoting Public-Private Partnerships for the 21st Century* (2015); *Beyond the Bedtime Story: Promoting Reading Development during the Middle School Years* (2015); *Betwixt and Between: Understanding and Meeting the Social and Emotional Developmental Needs of Students during the Middle School Transition Years* (2014); *Learning Style Perspectives: Impact upon the Classroom* (3rd ed., 2014); *Collapsing Educational Boundaries from Preschool to PhD: Building Bridges Across the Educational Spectrum* (2013); *Transforming Special Education Practices: A Primer for School Administrators and Policy Makers* (2012); and *Powerful Partners in Student Success: Schools, Families and Communities* (2012). He also co-authored several children's books, including *Yes, Mama* (2018), and the popular series *I Am Full of Possibilities*. Dr. Young may be contacted directly at nyoung1191@aol.com.

Professor **Kristen Bonanno-Sotiropoulos**, MS, has worked in education at various levels for more than a dozen years. Her professional career within K–12 public education included roles as a special education teacher and a special education administrator at the elementary- and middle-school levels. After her tenure in K–12, she transitioned to higher education to teach undergraduate and graduate courses as an assistant professor of special education at Springfield College, located in Springfield, Massachusetts. She is currently the assistant professor and coordinator of the Special Education Graduate Programs at Bay Path University. Professor Bonanno-Sotiropoulos received her bachelor of science in liberal studies and elementary education with academic distinction, as well as a master's degree of science in moderate disabilities from Bay Path University. She is currently an EdD candidate in the area of educational leadership and supervision, at American International College, where she is focusing her research on evidenced-based special education practices. Her current research interests include, amongst other areas, effective instructional programs and practices to assist learning disabled students with meeting rigorous academic expectations at all academic levels from preschool to college.

Professor Bonanno-Sotiropoulos has become a regular presenter at regional and national conferences and co-authored a series of book chapters related to the unique needs of struggling readers, as well as how higher education institutions can assist special needs students in making a successful transition to college. In addition, she has co-authored *Guardian of the Next Generation: Igniting the Passion for Quality Teaching* (in-press); *Wrestling with Writing: Effective Strategies for Struggling Students* (2018); *Paving the Pathway for Educational Success: Effective Classroom Interventions for Students with Learning Disabilities* (2018); and *Making the Grade: Promoting Positive Outcomes for Students with Learning Disabilities* (2018). She can be reached at kbsotiropoulos@baypath.edu.

Attorney **Jennifer A. Smolinski** has worked in education for more than three years. Her role within higher education includes the creation and directing of the Center for Disability Services and Academic Accommodations at American International College located in Springfield, Massachusetts. She has also taught criminal justice and legal research and writing classes within the field of higher education. Prior to her work at the collegiate level, Attorney Smolinski worked as a solo practitioner conducting education and disability advocacy as well as representing clients in real estate and business matters.

Attorney Smolinski received a bachelor of arts in anthropology and a bachelor of arts in sociology from the University of Connecticut, a master's degree in psychology and counseling, a master's degree in higher education student affairs from Salem State University, and a law degree from Massachusetts School of Law. She is currently an EdD in Educational Leadership and Supervision candidate at American International College, where she is focusing her research on special education and laws to protect students with disabilities in the classroom.

Attorney Smolinski has become a regular presenter educating the faculty, staff, and students at institutes of higher education on disabilities and accommodations at the collegiate level and has presented to local high school special education departments on the transition to college under the Americans with Disabilities Act. She is a co-author of *Captivating Classrooms: Student*

Engagement at the Heart of School Improvement (in-press); *Guardian of the Next Generation: Igniting the Passion for Quality Teaching* (in-press); *Making the Grade: Promoting Positive Outcomes for Students with Learning Disabilities* (2018). She can be reached at Jennifer.Smolinski@aic.edu.

Made in the USA
Middletown, DE
13 May 2018